Cesare Borgia
in a Nutshell

Cesare Borgia
in a Nutshell

M
MadeGlobal Publishing

For more information on
MadeGlobal Publishing, visit our website:
www.madeglobal.com

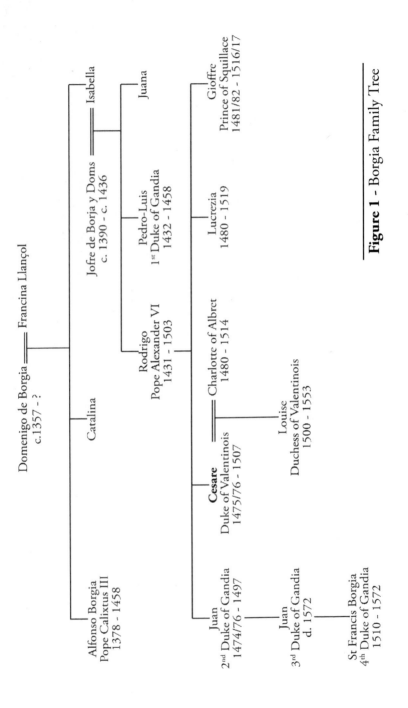

Figure 1 - Borgia Family Tree

Contents

Figure 2 - Portrait of Gentleman.
Thought to be Cesare Borgia
by Meloni Altobello (1490-1491 / 1543)
Museum Accademia Carrara

Introduction

In today's modern age everyone loves a good story steeped in drama and intrigue. The populace also loves stories based on real life, reading stories about their favourite celebrities in the news. Such behaviour has always been a part of the human mind-set – people love a good gossip. And as such salacious and dramatic stories have filtered down to us through the centuries to shock and astound us, and are often used in modern day television adaptations. Such adaptations are, of course, based on historical fact but draw on rumour and false propaganda as a means of "sexing" up the historical record. One such historical family that has suffered thanks to this is that of the Borgias – even during their lifetime, they were often tarred by their enemies, the proverbial whispers following their every move about murder, poisoning, orgies and incest.

The name of Borgia has become synonymous with murder, intrigue and incest – an ideal that remains 500 years after the death of Cesare Borgia. Cesare Borgia is at the centre of these ideas, and in the middle of the legend surrounding the Borgia name. From his earliest days in the church, Cesare Borgia was at the centre of a world that spun with back-stabbing and political intrigue, and part of a world in which his family name had already been dragged through the mud. It was the same with every great family before, during and after the Renaissance – if a family had power, there would be dissenters just waiting in the wings to spread malicious gossip. The Borgias were no different. As a family right at the heart of the seat of Christendom, simony was rife. Rodrigo Borgia benefitted from his uncle, Calixtus III, showing him special favour and Rodrigo, in turn, showed the same favour towards his own family once he secured his election as pope.

Cesare grew from cardinal to the most feared warlord in Italy at the time. The fear that he inspired in others certainly wasn't unfounded – he was an exceptional soldier, astutely politically minded and certainly unafraid of making enemies. Because of this, his ever-growing ambition and the threat he posed not only to politics within Italy but to countries beyond their borders, the rumour mill began to churn and other political factions took notice. They began to write things down, to twist things to their own means. And, as such, the legend of an evil man who murdered for sport and slept with his sister was born.

Why then has the legend of Cesare Borgia as an evil man stuck? Murder and illicit sexual activities were the norms in Renaissance Italy, and in fact, violence was a part of everyday life. Rulers of individual states came from families who had built their seats of power upon incredibly violent conquests: the Sforzas were famous condottieri, founded by Muzio Attendolo Sforza; Sigismondo Malatesta, the Wolf of Rimini, was famous for having killed his wives; the Pazzi famously murdered Girolamo De Medici in Florence. There are many other examples of violence both from the ruling classes and in the streets, but none of these has stayed within the public imagination quite as much as Cesare's acts of violence. Perhaps this was because Cesare Borgia deliberately exploited his fearful image and permitted the stories about him to circulate. It allowed for a greater impact. And, thus, it allowed for the populace to grow ever more terrified and shocked at the actions of one man who knew how to twist things to his own advantage.

The idea of Cesare being in love with his sister Lucrezia is an idea that has also become ingrained within the public imagination. From historical fiction to historical television drama, the story of the incestuous relationship between Cesare and Lucrezia is told time and again. But how much truth is there to this? It should be noted that incest has been prevalent throughout history, with royal houses inbreeding to keep their bloodlines pure. Yet for the Borgia family it seems to have been one topic that their enemies clung on to as a way of making the family seem debauched and corrupt – it was the perfect way of vilifying the family even more than they already had been. Yet it is often forgotten that many of the great Italian families were also accused of committing incest – one such example being the Wolf of Rimini, who was said to have committed incest with both his son and his daughter. Of course, sexual misdeeds were the norm – cardinals and popes were known to have mistresses and bastard children while many lay-people also had mistresses as well as large numbers of illegitimate children. It was the cultural norm, so much so that bastards of noble and even royal descent were brought up alongside legitimate heirs of the court.

The legend of the evil and corrupt Borgia family, a family of Marrano, has sprung up simply from the reports and pages of those who wrote of them at the time. The anti-Borgia faction wished to sully the name of such a powerful family, and what better way to do so than by taking rumours and running with them? Of course, there must have been some basis in fact for at least some of it. That way, with a grain of truth, it made the rumours seem all the more believable. By drawing on Cesare's violent acts as a soldier, on his close relationship with his sister, it would have been all too easy to bypass the activities of the family that were less salacious and, as such, the myth of the evil Borgia dynasty has come down to us throughout the years.

It is, however, important to look at what lies behind the myth. Thanks to a number of sources written at the time, it can be difficult to get beyond the bias that has survived, but it is possible. Historians have come a long way in disseminating the differences between myth and fact. However, the presumption still remains that the Borgia family were nothing more than incestuous, murdering tyrants. This can at least partly be blamed on popular media, on historical fiction and television shows.

This book does not aim to be a long biography of Cesare Borgia. Instead, it is a brief history of the man and the life that he lived to those interested in learning about the reality behind the myths and rumours. To begin, we must of course start at the beginning; that is to say by looking at the world into which Cesare Borgia was born. From there, his life through to his death can be looked at, along with the most important events that shaped the legend of Cesare Borgia as it stands today.

Setting the stage and early life

Rome, at the time when the Borgia family came into power, was a city that was finally regaining its footing. At one point in its long history, Rome had been the centre of an empire – it was the epicentre of a powerful people whose influence spread across the world. But by the fifteenth century, the once magnificent city was in decline, with even the pope having abandoned the city for Avignon in 1305. The papacy did not return until 1377. Previous efforts to bring the papacy back to the Eternal City had been in vain – for years the Avignon popes refused to listen to the calls for them to return to Rome, which had been described as the "rubbish heap of history". Pope Urban V, elected in 1362, was the first pope to return to Rome since the move to Avignon. He arrived in 1367, shocked and appalled at the state of this once great city. It was dilapidated, its once magnificent monuments crumbling and the palaces of both the Vatican and the Lateran had fallen into disrepair. Urban, because of the state of the city, only stayed in Rome for three years. But during those years he began a series of building works in an effort to bring the city back to magnificence, including an impressive project to rebuild the Lateran[1]. In just three years Urban brought back some of the people's faith in both the Roman Catholic Church and in Rome, the seat of the Roman Catholic faith. Urban was dead just one year after leaving Rome, in 1370. It was whispered that his death had come about because he had not heeded the warnings of Birgitta Gudmarsson, an elderly woman who sat begging for alms by the front doors of the convent of San Lorenzo. She said she had been granted a vision from Christ while living in Sweden, telling her to travel to Rome, and that she would remain there until she witnessed the return of the papacy. Birgitta did not live to see the return of the papacy to the Eternal City. She died in 1373 and Pope Gregory XI brought the church back to the city in 1377.

Following the return to Rome, the city once more began to return to greatness despite the corruption that was rife in the church. Rome was at the centre of the Papal States, an area of land in which the people paid deference and rental to the pope. Surrounding the Papal States were other states ruled over by other lords. To the south was the large kingdom of Naples, and to the east and the north it was bordered by the Republic of Florence, the Republic of Siena and the Duchy of Ferrara. Each state was completely independent of the other but the larger states – Venice, Milan, the Papal States – used the smaller states as political pawns. But Rome was literally at the centre of it all. Geographically it was situated within the centre of all the surrounding states and spiritually it was at the centre of the Catholic world. And despite the power of the surrounding states, the pope held sway over the ruling families. Popes held absolute power over their subjects and lived like kings, but more importantly they held the fear of excommunication above the heads of the secular rulers of Italy, like the Sword of Damocles. If the pope made the decision to excommunicate one of the ruling families, they would be cut off and open to attack while their allies were forbidden by religious law from helping them. Such was the power of the popes, making the Papal States the most powerful in Italy, despite other states having better military and more financial backing.

But the road to the papacy, as is the case today, was a long one. To become pope you had to first be a member of the College of Cardinals and, as such, every powerful family in Italy wanted one of their sons, usually the younger, to become a cardinal. It was a stepping-stone, via years of accumulated wealth and power through various benefices to the highest religious seat in the world. The way to the throne of St Peter was rife with corruption, however, which was something that many opponents of the Catholic Church would bring up time and again, each election involved cardinals buying votes as a way to make sure that they won the papal tiara, something that was evident in the election of Pope Alexander VI.

It was into this world, a world of corruption and petty politics, that Cesare Borgia was born.

Cesare Borgia, bastard son of Cardinal Rodrigo Borgia and the courtesan Vanozza dei Cattanei, was born in Rome at some point between September 1475 and April 1476. Unfortunately, as is often the case, we do not know his exact date of birth. Cesare's mother Vanozza was actually married to a man by the name of Domenico Gianozzo for the sheer sake of appearances, and they had been married some time before Cesare was born[2]. Vanozza had, however, been Rodrigo's mistress for at least two years previous to the marriage, so there was no doubt whatsoever that Cesare was Rodrigo's son.

The Borgia family was originally from Spain, until in 1444 Cesare's great-uncle, Alonso, travelled to Rome to become a cardinal. As was typical of many families of nobility at the time, the Borgia family (or Borja, as is the Spanish spelling of the Zaragoza town from whence they came) stated that they were descended from the Aragonese royal family. Alfonso was appointed to the post of private secretary of King Alfonso V of Aragon, a post he would keep for the next forty-two years. Thanks to his work, which included helping to arrange the abdication of Antipope

Clement VIII and thus paving the way for the ending of the Great Schism, Alfonso was awarded a cardinal's hat. He was elected as pope in 1455 and became Pope Calixtus III. One of his first vows was to organise a massive crusade against Constantinople, in which he would free the city from the Turks. Calixtus was determined to see this through, which surprised many given his age and the fact that he suffered from painful attacks of gout. He managed to raise enough money by raising taxes, pawning off his own mitre, selling works of art and even stopping restoration work around Rome to build a fleet of ships for his holy crusade. Calixtus also showed special favour to members of his family. His nephew, Rodrigo Borgia, was appointed as vice-chancellor of the Holy See. This was a post that Rodrigo would hold right up until he became pope. The special favour shown to Rodrigo, while not unusual for the time period, was something Rodrigo would carry on with his own family once he was elected as Pope Alexander VI in 1492.[3]

Rodrigo Borgia, however, was in his youth an incredibly handsome young man with boundless energy. He had a great sense of humour but got bored very easily, and he loved, more than anything, beautiful women. Rodrigo never attempted to conceal his love of women, even when he became Pope Alexander VI and took Giulia Farnese as his mistress. He was also a man to be reckoned with as he would prove time and again as pope.

Vanozza dei Cattanei went on to bear Rodrigo three more children after Cesare, the names of which are synonymous with the infamous Borgia family: Lucrezia; Juan (Giovanni); and Jofre – although Rodrigo at first did not recognise Jofre as his own[4]. The children were not brought up in their fathers' house. As Rodrigo was a cardinal, it would not be seemly for him to fully acknowledge his illegitimate children. Cesare and Juan were brought up together in the same house, both with their own household, as would befit sons of the Church, whereas Lucrezia spent the first years of her life with her mother before moving to the house of her father's first cousin, Adriana De Mila. The children, of course, saw much of their father, as he loved them dearly, and Rodrigo planned fully for his sons' futures. Juan was destined to be a soldier while Cesare would go into the Church[5]. Jofre, however, would be used as a pawn by his father in marriage treaties to form alliances, normal for the youngest son of a powerful family, and Lucrezia, of course, would take up a good marriage. They were a tight family unit, and both Cesare and Lucrezia inherited from Rodrigo his resilience, strength and, to some extent, his good spirits. Cesare was described as having a "head most beautiful", and while there is no surviving contemporary portrait, the one that does exist and is said to be of Cesare shows a young man with a startling resemblance to his mother.[6]

Juan, however, was seen as an exceptionally spoiled child and was described by the Aragonese chronicler Zurita as "the spoiled boy"[7]. He was said to have looked a lot like Cesare, except his hair was lighter. He was handsome, incredibly vain and self-indulgent, lacking Cesare's self-control. It was an attitude that would earn him many enemies and eventually lead to his death. Lucrezia, however, was exceptionally beautiful and good-natured, the "darling of the family". Both Cesare and his father adored her and her feminine, intelligent charm.

Rodrigo did not just have children by Vanozza, however. Pedro Luis was born in 1462, Isabella in 1467, and Girolama in 1470 – all three had different mothers thanks to Rodrigo's many mistresses. It must be noted that it was only Vanozza's children who were part of a tight family unit with their father. Cesare, Juan, Lucrezia and Jofre would not have known their elder siblings very well at all. In fact, by the time Cesare was just eight years old, both Pedro Luis and Girolama were dead. Vanozza's brood, however, were incredibly close-knit, and their lives were dominated by their father.

Cesare would have started his education at an early age where he learnt Greek, Italian, French, Latin, arithmetic, geometry, music and drawing. Of course, he could already speak and write Spanish, having grown up in a Spanish-speaking home, and he would continue to speak in Spanish when around his family as he grew older. An important part of education at the time was physical exercise, something Cesare excelled at as a young boy and continued to excel at throughout his life. He shared a passion for hunting with his father, learned bullfighting and was fiercely competitive in everything he did.

As early as 1481, at the age of just 6, Cesare was holding church benefices. At the age of 7, he was made apostolic prothonotary by Sixtus IV, and in July 1482, he was given a canonry in his father's bishopric of Valencia as well as becoming archdeacon of Jatvia and rector of Gandia.[8] While he was not yet of an age to take an active part in these benefices, the money went straight to Rodrigo for Cesare's maintenance and education. For a child not yet eight years old, it is an almost unseemly amount of church benefices to hold. But for a son destined to go into the Church, such things were normal. It was a stepping-stone towards gaining the much sought after cardinal's hat. By the age of 14, when he became a man, and for the next three years, Cesare would attend and complete his education at the Universities of Perugia and Pisa. At Perugia, he would see his first experience of harsh political life, and his eyes would open to the true position of how things stood in the states of the Church. Here he would also meet a man who would later become his condottiere, Gian Paulo of the unruly Baglioni family. In 1491, Cesare received more benefices that would advance his career in the church. In September, he received the bishopric of Pamplona, the ancient capital of Navarre, and he was only 15. It caused an uproar with the people in his new bishopric as he had not yet taken holy orders. They believed the only reason he was given the bishopric was because of his father, the cardinal.[9] Rodrigo tried to calm them, saying Cesare was given the bishopric based on his merits, while Cesare wrote a hasty letter to them, giving them a representative of his to look after them. Yet the people of Navarre remained rebellious until Pope Innocent intervened. Innocent sent an admonition to the people of Pamplona, against all those who rebelled against the bishopric and took its revenues for their own. The admonition seems to have worked – after all, one did not argue with the pope without risking the worst of all punishments: excommunication.

After two years in Perugia, Cesare went to the University of Pisa, where he studied for his doctorate in law. This was also the territory of the powerful Medici family, and Rodrigo wanted to be on good terms with them. Rodrigo wrote to Lorenzo De' Medici (the Magnificent), asking that Cesare be placed under his protection. Lorenzo's second son Giovanni was also destined for the church, yet the two did not end up being friends. This was mainly down to the style in which Cesare lived, as well as the rivalry between the two boys. Cesare lived so ostentatiously that he outshone the other noble families, including the Medicis. Cesare was also a brilliant student, whereas Giovanni was not so much. Cesare was awarded his doctorate long before Giovanni, and thus it is likely that Giovanni resented the bastard son of the Spanish cardinal. Yet Giovanni was awarded a place in the College of Cardinals long before Cesare was given his hat – Giovanni was a legitimate child and no bastard could take up a seat in the college. But despite their rivalry and despite Giovanni likely seeing Cesare as an upstart in the eyes of legitimate Italian nobility, when Lorenzo the Magnificent died in 1492, Cesare wrote to the Medici family to express his condolences. It is likely that this was a political move rather than a personal one – after all, the death of such a powerful man would mean great changes in the political world of Renaissance Italy.

In 1492, Pope Innocent's health began to decline, and this was Rodrigo's hour to shine. Innocent was so unwell that he could not eat, and the only nourishment he had was human milk. Stories, of course, flew around the city of Rome about the ways and means used to try and help the dying pope. One such story involved a Jewish doctor giving the pope the blood of three young boys – and all three boys died from exsanguination.[10] True or not, it was certainly a story that took Rome by storm and is one of the many dramatic stories that have filtered down to us today. The cardinals gathered around Innocent's death-bed, and reports came from ambassadors about the fights that erupted at his bedside. The Mantuan ambassador reported on the childish quarrels of Rodrigo Borgia and Giuliano della Rovere, with della Rovere reminding the dying pope of Rodrigo's Spanish heritage, while Rodrigo reportedly lost his temper at the slur.

On 22 July 1492, Pope Innocent was dead, and the cardinals went into conclave. At this point Cesare would have been kept abreast of the news from Rome, knowing that his family's future hung in the balance. At the age of 61, this was Rodrigo's last chance at the papacy, although his success certainly wasn't definite. Rodrigo had little to no support, and his Spanish blood was seen as a huge set-back. Politics would also have a part to play in the election. The twenty-five cardinals who found themselves locked in conclave were mainly of two political factions – one was headed by Giuliano della Rovere, who was determined to keep Rodrigo away from the papacy at all costs. This faction was supported by the French, as well as the powerful Venetian state and the powerful families of Colonna and Savelli. The other faction was led by Ascanio Sforza, Ludovico 'Il Moro' Sforza's brother, and represented the interests of the Milanese state. Sforza supported Borgia as papal candidate, thanks to them being old political allies and friends, and opposed the pro-French stance of della Rovere and his cardinals.

This was when Rodrigo played his cards and the infamous corruption so well-known of papal elections at the time began to show. He offered various offices to his colleagues and to pay them off. There is one story of four mules loaded with gold and silver seen moving from Rodrigo's palace in Rome to Cardinal Ascanio Sforza's palace, and Sforza was also offered the vice-chancellorship.[11] On 11 August, thanks to his wheeling and dealing, Rodrigo Borgia was elected as pope. And the next morning a courier brought the news to Cesare who hurried back to Pisa to await his father's orders. Ten days later he was at the Castle of Spoleto. Although he did not attend his father's coronation, his new life was about to begin and, at the tender age of 18, despite his bastard blood, he was made cardinal, much to the upset of the church.

Figure 3 - Pope Alexander VI
by Cristofano dell'Altissimo (1525–1605)

From cardinal to soldier

Following Rodrigo Borgia's ascension to the Throne of St Peter as Pope Alexander VI, Cesare Borgia was kept out of Rome on his father's orders. He stayed in Spoleto for a few months. His father certainly hadn't forgotten him, however, and within a week of his ascension Cesare was given the archbishopric of Valencia worth 16,000 ducats per year. Just a few months after the ascension, all of the Borgia children were back in Rome, and when Cesare returned he took up residence in a grand palace in the Borgo, a newly built quarter around the Vatican. The 17-year-old Cesare, though, seemingly had the good sense not to let his new importance go to his head, unlike his brother Juan who certainly wasn't being modest and spent much of his time in the limelight. Even at such an early stage in his career, Cesare had no inclination towards the priesthood and Boccaccio commented that his manner was that of "a son of a great Prince; above all he is merry and fond of society".[12]

Both Cesare and Juan had their places in their father's plans and by early February 1493, the pope's plans for his sons were becoming evident. Rumours abounded that Juan, Duke of Gandia, would be made gonfalonier of the papal armies and Cesare would be made a cardinal. The main issue that Alexander had to deal with in making Cesare a cardinal was the issue of his illegitimacy. So, on 20 September 1493, he issued a papal bull stating that Cesare was, in fact, the legitimate son of Vanozza dei Cattanei and her husband, Domenico. On the same day, he issued a secret bull testifying that Cesare was his own son.[13] This meant that the cardinals Pallavicini and Orsini, who had been examining Cesare's status, could say that he was legitimate and thus eligible to join the College of Cardinals. As should have been expected, Cesare's joining of the college caused an uproar – when Giuliano della Rovere (later Pope Julius II) heard the news, he gave a massive yell of rage and took to his bed with a fever, saying he would not allow the college to be so abused.[14] Cesare was barely 18 years old when he was invested into his cardinal robes and still hadn't taken holy orders. And the main reason behind Giuliano's rage was that he and his followers believed the new nominations, not only of Alexander's son but also that of Ippolito D'Este who was not yet 15, and Alessandro Farnese, the brother of Alexander's mistress Giulia, were a move by the pope to fill the college with non-Italians. The college voted in consistory on 20 September, and the decision was close – ten cardinals opposed allowing the nominees in, while eleven agreed with the pope. On 17 October, Cesare made a formal entry into Rome to take up his seat as Cardinal of Valencia and counsellor to his father.

For a long time, Cesare stayed by his father's side working on church business and supporting his father in family business. Juan Borgia had left Rome in August that year and travelled to the Spanish court of Isabela of Castile and Ferdinand of Aragon, where he married Maria Enriquez, Ferdinand's own cousin. While Juan was in Spain, Alexander received reports of Juan's misbehaviour, his poor treatment of his new wife, non-consummation of his marriage and gambling. The reports of non-consummation were not true, as Maria was soon pregnant, but the other reports were, and Cesare joined his father in writing to Juan. From Orvieto

Cesare wrote, saying that while he didn't really believe the reports, he advised Juan to make sure only good reports came back to them.[15]

1494 was a year that proved to be huge for Italy. Until that point, Italy had been under threat of invasion from Charles VIII of France over the country of Naples. Charles had his eye on Naples for a long time, believing that it belonged to France. When King Ferrante of Naples died in January 1494, Charles sent an envoy to Rome saying that if the pope favoured Ferrante's son Alfonso over himself, then there would be trouble. Charles had also been in talks with della Rovere. On 17 March, Charles officially announced that he would invade Italy and, despite the cardinals who opposed Alexander fleeing to Charles's side, Alexander kept on strengthening his bonds with Naples. Agreement was reached between the pope and Alfonso of Naples. Alfonso would be crowned King of Naples, and little Jofre was married to Sancia, given the title of Prince of Squillace and 40,000 ducats as an annual income.[16] Yet the threat of France did not go away, and by 18 December 1494, the French were in Rome. Cesare waited in the Vatican with his father. On Christmas Day, Alexander told the cardinals that he decided to admit the French king into Rome, and that night three envoys arrived in the city. Now all Cesare and Alexander could do was wait for Charles to enter the city. He chose his moment on 31 December, St Silvester's Day and talks began. Charles demanded that Cesare accompany him on his trip to Naples and that the Castel Sant Angelo be handed over to him. The pope refused, invoking the French king's wrath, and Cesare, Alexander and four cardinals fled through the underground passages from the Vatican to the Castello. On 10 January, the pope capitulated after a section of the Castello walls collapsed and killed three guards. On 15 January, an agreement was signed: Cesare would go with Charles to Naples for three months, free passage was to be allowed throughout the Papal States and a pardon was to be given to the churchmen and nobles who had rebelled against the pope. On 28 January, Charles, Cesare and the army set out for Naples, and it is during this trip that we see the first signs of the infamous Cesare. On the 30 January, just two days later, while guests of della Rovere at Velletri, Charles received news that Cesare Borgia was missing, that he had escaped dressed as a groom of the royal stables. It was said that he travelled so quickly that he was able to stay that night in Rome. He ended up going to Spoleto the next day. Charles flew into a rage, screaming, "All Italians are dirty dogs and the Holy Father is as bad as the worst of them!"[17] The pope denied he had anything to do with his son's escape, but it can be imagined that the escape was secretly agreed between them before Cesare had even left. More bad news was to get to Charles, though, when it was found that the chests taken on the journey had been emptied of their gold and jewels. This daring escape was one that would set Cesare up nicely for his future career, showing all the hallmarks he would become famous for: disguise; secrecy; as well as a location very cleverly picked to snub both the French king and della Rovere.

The years 1494-95 were a huge learning curve for Cesare in which he gained first-hand experience of politics. He had seen the power of the French army and had watched as the Kingdom of Naples fell before the might of France. He had also watched as his father outplayed the French, despite the young king having a massive army at his back. By this point, Cesare was just 20 years old, and his career was just getting started – although in other ways, it was also ending and a new chapter would begin for the young Borgia. He had gained a sense of power and an innate fascination with military tactics, and it was following this that Cesare Borgia would make his move.

The rivalry between Cesare and his brother Juan is the stuff of legend. After all, Juan was the son destined for the military, the son who had been made gonfalonier of the papal armies, and that was everything Cesare wanted. Instead, he was stuck in cardinal robes. In August 1496, Juan returned to Rome from Spain, leaving his pregnant wife and young son where they were. He arrived dressed ostentatiously, with a hat hung with pearls as well as a

Turkish mantle hung with gold brocade. He had not outgrown his
love of nice clothes, it seemed. The prodigal son had returned and
just one month after his arrival it was reported that "these sons of
the Pope are consumed with envy of each other". Alexander doted
on Juan, despite the fact that he relied on Cesare. But with Juan
back in the picture, Cesare was no longer his father's only right-
hand man.

But Juan Borgia was not as militarily astute as his brother
would prove to be. Following his return from Spain, Alexander
decided that it was time to deal with the problem of the Orsini
family. They had been a thorn in the side of the papacy for far too
long. The lands of both the Orsini and Colonna families lay to the
north and south of Rome, essentially surrounding the city. So if
any enemies of the papacy wished to make their way into Rome,
all they had to do was bribe the Orsini and Colonna family. It
was a risk Alexander wasn't willing to take. Now, with the French
gone and Virginio Orsini locked up, it was the perfect time to
strike.[18] And as luck would have it, the Colonna family were in the
pockets of the papacy at that moment and willing to fight in the
papal armies.

Alexander sent two men to lead the attack against the Orsini
strongholds. Guidobaldo de Montefeltro would command the
troops, and Juan Borgia, Duke of Gandia, would be his second-in-
command. Montefeltro was weak, and Borgia was inexperienced
on the battlefield. With such commanders, failure was inevitable.
Despite the initial success of the campaign, with ten castles falling
within two months of the campaign's start, it was in December
1496 when the whole thing started to unravel. Montefeltro and
Borgia began a siege of the castle at Bracciano – Montefeltro was
wounded, which meant that Juan Borgia had to carry on alone.
Borgia's lack of success and his inexperience was the subject of
mockery to the Orsinis, and they sent a donkey into Borgia's camp
with a sign hung around its neck that read: "I am the ambassador
of the Duke of Gandia".[19] A letter was also found placed within the
donkey's backside. The rest of the campaign was a disappointment

for the papal forces too. In January 1497, Juan Borgia fled the battlefield of Sorano, having lost 500 men and all of the artillery that he had brought with him to the battle.[20]

On 8 June 1497, Alexander announced two new appointments for his sons. Cesare was made legate for the coronation of the new King of Naples, while Juan was given the Duchy of Benevento as well as the cities of Terracina and Pontecorvo.[21] This caused resentment, and Juan became the target of anti-Borgia hostility, particularly from the Orsini family after Juan was involved in an initiative to take back the Orsini lands. Just one week later, on 14 June, Juan disappeared. That very afternoon Cesare and Juan had ridden to have supper with their mother, returning as night was falling. As they reached the bridge leading to the Castel Sant Angelo, Juan told his brother that he must leave them and go elsewhere on his own. According to a report given later, both Juan and Cesare's servants tried to tell him not to go alone, but to no avail. Juan was adamant. All he did was send a groom back for his light armour. After he had taken his leave, a masked man got on a mule behind Juan, and they rode off. Juan's groom was attacked on his way to the Vatican to get Juan's armour, but returned to wait for his master despite his stab wounds.

Another version of events states that less than an hour after Juan had dismissed him, the groom was attacked and horrifically wounded. He was discovered lying in a pool of blood and dragged into a nearby house. The owner of the house was apparently so frightened that she refused to report what had happened until the following day. Other reports state that, although the groom was attacked on his way to fetch Juan's armour, the wounds were mild so he arrived at the piazza to wait for his master, and returned to the palace thinking that Juan had spent the night with a woman, as he so often did. Thus the incident was not reported that night to the pope. The next morning, Juan's servants told the pope that he had not returned, but Alexander was not overly worried because Juan often did such things and was known for his amours. Worry began to set in as the day wore on and in the evening Cesare was

summoned before his father to tell him where Juan was. Cesare
told him what had happened to the groom and the pope panicked,
ordering a search to be made.

On the 16 June, enquiries began to be made when a fisherman
by the name of Giorgio Schiavi reported that he had seen a body
thrown into the Tiber by two men. He was asked why he had
not reported it sooner, and Schiavi retorted that he saw bodies
being thrown into the river all the time. "In the course of my
life, on various nights, I have seen more than a hundred bodies
thrown into the river right at this spot, and never heard of anyone
troubling himself about them."[22] Following the report, all the
boatmen of Rome were ordered to search the river and were
promised a reward. At around midday, the body of a young man
was pulled from the River Tiber near the Church of Santa Maria
Del Popolo. The body was fully clothed, with his gloves still on,
and a purse hanging from his belt contained 30 ducats. Nine stab
wounds were counted on the body, across the neck, chest and legs
– it was the body of Juan Borgia, Duke of Gandia.[23]

Johannes Burchard recounts Alexander VI's reaction to the
death of his son in his diaries:

> When the Pope heard that the Duke was dead and
> thrown into the river like dung, he fell into a paroxysm
> of grief, and such was the anguish and bitterness in his
> heart that he locked himself away in his room and
> wailed with abandon.[24]

Juan's body was taken to the Castel Sant Angelo, where he was
cleaned up and dressed in military uniform as befitted his status as
the Duke of Gandia and gonfalonier of the papal armies. He was
then taken to the Church of Santa Maria del Popolo, where he was
entombed – the church itself had links to the Borgia family long
after his death when his mother Vanozza was buried there. The
procession was led by over 100 torchbearers and members of his
household. According to one observer at the funeral, Juan looked
even more handsome in death than he had in life.[25]

Understandably, Alexander VI was distraught and, according to reports, shut himself up for days, refusing to eat or drink. On 19 June, once he had recovered, the pope made a solemn announcement regarding the murder of his son:

> *The Duke of Gandia is dead. A greater calamity could not have befallen us for we bore him unbounded affection. Life has lost all interest for us. It must be that God punishes us for our sins, for the Duke has done nothing to deserve so terrible a fate.*[26]

Rumours flew around the city: who had killed Juan Borgia, Duke of Gandia? The Orsinis were blamed due to the recent fighting as well as the Duke of Urbino, who had the motive of revenge for his imprisonment during the Orsini war, and the Sforza family, who were absolved of the crime. A week later, though, the search for Juan's murderer was called off, perhaps because the Borgia family had found out who had committed the crime and wanted it kept quiet. Bad blood between Cesare and Juan was mentioned by various envoys, and the strange masked man is mentioned in all contemporary accounts of what happened. At the time, though, Cesare was not immediately thought of, and blame lay mainly on the Orsini family. A year later, however, rumours started in Venice that Cesare was responsible – although it should be noted that the Orsini had many friends in Venice. The story began to take form as it spread and it was said that Cesare was so jealous of his brother's position and that Lucrezia had more affection for Juan that he had him killed and thrown into the Tiber. But was Cesare capable of killing his own brother? Although he gained massively from his brother's death, there is absolutely no contemporary evidence to support that Cesare was responsible. The story rests on rumours of alleged jealousy, the supposed incestuous relationship with Lucrezia, and the fact that Cesare profited from the death of his brother. No contemporary accounts at all point the finger of blame at Cesare.[27]

In fact, Cesare did not benefit from Juan's death for over a year, and he remained in the church until 17 August 1498, when he resigned as a cardinal and embarked on a secular career in the military.

Figure 4 - The fire place in the Borgia apartments, bearing Alexander VI's name.
Photo © Samantha Morris

Figure 5 - Portrait of Juan Borgia (1474–1497)

The path to marriage

Following Cesare's departure from the church and into the secular lifestyle, Alexander VI began looking for a wife for his son. Obviously, as a cardinal, he was not allowed to marry. But now he had formally resigned his cardinal's hat, he had an important job to do – make alliances for the good of the Papal States. This had been planned since before Cesare left for Naples to crown King Federico. But while Cesare was in Naples, playing at being peacemaker and discussing dynastic marriages for his sister as well as taking over his now dead brother's estates in the area, he began to take delight in the pleasures of Naples. It is rumoured that while there he fell in love with a woman named Maria Diaz Garlon and spent the huge sum of 20,000 ducats just to win her favour. Yet Cesare was already proving to be a hugely extravagant man who loved luxury, a luxury that King Federico of Naples had to bear with Cesare as his guest.[28]

Cesare also managed to pick up a long lasting souvenir of his trip to Naples – he had come down with syphilis, known as the "French Disease" to many and the "Naples Disease" after

Charles VIII's army picked it up, or perhaps spread it between the people and themselves, during their stay in the city. But within a few months of getting back to Rome, Cesare would have probably considered himself cured as the first stage of syphilis, with its unsightly rashes, lasts between ten and ninety days. It was a disease that would haunt him for the rest of his life, though.[29]

After returning to Rome on 5 September 1497 and meeting his with his father, it was decided that the hopes of a Borgia dynasty now rested on Cesare's shoulders. But, at this point, Cesare was still a cardinal and could not marry. The answer was a simple one. Cesare would renounce the cardinalate, and Alexander VI would find his son a wife. There were even rumours of marrying Cesare off to his brother's widow, Sancia, and making young Jofre a cardinal instead.

Following his sister's divorce from Giovanni Sforza, which was formally agreed in December 1497, rumours would fly around Cesare once more. A man known as Perotto (Pedro Calderon), one of Alexander's Spanish chamberlains, mysteriously disappeared, and it was thought in February 1498 that the young man was in prison for getting Lucrezia pregnant. By 14 February, it was apparent this was not the case. He had been thrown into the Tiber.[30] Burchard mentions the incident in his diaries:

> Perotto, who last Thursday, the 8th of this month, fell not of his own will into the Tiber, was fished up today in that river.

It appeared that Lucrezia and Perotto had been involved in an affair, and nine months before Perotto's death Lucrezia went and stayed in the convent of San Sisto, apparently exiled for her bad behaviour. Was she pregnant with Perotto's child at this time? Was she whisked away to the convent to hide her misconduct at a time when her father and brother wanted to prove her virginity for the sake of her divorce? There were rumours also that the body of one of Lucrezia's women, Pantasilea, was found with Perotto – an act of vengeance or perhaps the removal of evidence of Lucrezia's misconduct. It did not take long for these deaths to be attributed to Cesare. He would allow nothing to stand in the way of his plans for his sister, especially since they were so entwined with his own, and the fact that he was so very close to her.

For a long time, Alexander pursued Naples for his son's bride, especially considering as how Lucrezia was married to Alfonso of Aragon this would only strengthen the ties between the two families. Yet that idea fell flat after Federico refused to consider transferring Juan's old estates to Cesare to compensate for his loss of church revenues. However, a different avenue was found, and Alexander sent envoys over to France to enter talks with King Charles VIII. This was interrupted when Charles died, but when his son Louis XII took over he had huge reasons for being on good terms with the pope – mainly because he wanted a divorce from his wife and only a papal dispensation could allow the dissolution of his marriage. Alexander jumped at the opportunity and in June 1498 sent envoys to France to get the marriage dissolved. It was also agreed that Cesare would go to France where he would try and ensnare Carlotta of Aragon, who was residing at the French court. Thus, on 17 August 1498, he officially announced his decision to resign as a cardinal. That same day, envoys from France arrived with the documents that would allow the former Cardinal of Valencia to call himself the Duc de Valentinois, and from henceforth would be known to the Italians as "Il Valentino".[31]

Before he left for France, it became obvious that Cesare was starting to worry about his looks. He was spending a lot of time in athletic sports, often violent ones, but he worried about his appearance especially when he started wearing grander and grander clothing to try and divert attention from his health issues. This was at a time when it would have been so important to make a good impression, especially with the prospect of a bride on the horizon. Secondary syphilis started to show itself on his body and, worryingly, his face – and he was only around the age of 23.[32] So little was known about this new venereal disease that the

likelihood of Cesare realising the unsightly rash would go away on
its own within a couple of months was slim.

On 1 October 1498, Cesare took formal leave of his father and
made his way to France. Burchard stated that Cesare's departure
was "without pomp", though this is only true in the fact that there
was no official leaving procession. Upon his departure, Cesare
was dressed in a white brocade tunic with a black velvet mantle
across his shoulders. His cap was adorned with rubies, and his
boots had gold chains and pearls sewn into them. His horse was
even dressed for the occasion, draped in red silk, gold brocade and
silver shoes. Cesare was accompanied by 100 squires, pages and
grooms as well as twelve baggage carts, fifty baggage mules and
some Spanish riding horses. And when he arrived, ostentatiously
dressed, he disgusted the French court. They were used to much
plainer clothing. In Italy, a person's outward appearance was
essential to show how important you were, but in France, this was
considered much less important. In fact, Cesare's time in France
would change his outward show of importance, and he would
dress in black velvet at a time when he was more sure of himself
than ever.[33]

The woman that Cesare had his eye on was Carlotta of
Aragon, and their meeting was not a comfortable one. She was
determined not to marry him and made no secret of it, saying she
did not want to be known as "La Cardinala" – and she was already
in love with another. But while he failed to win over his intended
bride, he won over the French court and the king considered
him an asset. Indeed, Louis tried to convince Carlotta to marry
Cesare, but she remained steadfast, saying she would not marry
Cesare Borgia unless her father willed it. When the Neapolitan
envoy arrived, and the issue of the marriage was pressed, the envoy
replied: "To a bastard son of the Pope, the King not only would
not give his legitimate daughter, but not even a bastard child."

The king made one last effort to persuade Carlotta to marry
Cesare. He invited her to dine alone with him. His efforts failed,
and Cesare talked of leaving France to return to Rome, although

this could potentially have been a way of placing pressure upon the king to find him a new bride.[34] After all, it was his first time away from his father in such a capacity, and he became the driving force behind the French alliance.

It was Louis XII who ended up finding Cesare his bride. Her name was Charlotte d'Albret, an exceptionally beautiful woman and kinswoman to the French queen. Cesare was very enthusiastic over the match but what Charlotte thought is not recorded – she probably didn't have much choice. The marriage negotiations went on for over six weeks. Charlotte's father was determined to get as much out of the marriage as possible, and demanded to see the dispensation that allowed Cesare to marry as well at the 100,00 livres promised as a dowry to be paid in ducats. By the end of April 1499, negotiations were brought to a successful end, and on 10 May, the agreement was signed in front of both the king and queen, with the king formally giving his consent to the marriage.[35] But what did Charlotte think of this marriage? Had she heard of the cruel Cesare Borgia who had committed atrocities in Italy? Had she heard the rumours that her future husband had committed fratricide? Whatever the answers to those questions, Charlotte d'Albret would have first seen the insulted suitor of Carlotta of Aragon, and it is likely that she went to the marriage unwillingly. Cesare would have to turn his charm on and make Charlotte love him.

On 12 May 1499, Cesare and Charlotte were married in the queen's closet at Blois. It consisted of a private ceremony followed by a huge court wedding feast. Huge silk tents were set up in the castle grounds for a massive feast. The usual lack of privacy before a marriage was consummated did of course happen, and the couple consummated their marriage that afternoon, and again that evening. It is said that Charlotte's ladies reported that Cesare was the victim of a practical joke in which he asked the apothecary for pills to pleasure his lady, but the apothecary gave him laxatives – Robert de la Marck wrote in his diary:

> *To tell you of the Duke of Valentinois' wedding night,*
> *he asked the apothecary for some pills to pleasure his*
> *lady, from whom he received a bad turn for, instead*
> *of giving him what he asked for, he gave him laxative*
> *pills, to such an effect that he never ceased going to*
> *the privy the whole night, as the ladies reported in the*
> *morning*[36].

Cesare could not stay off the privy for the whole night.

Whether this story is apocryphal or not, Cesare proudly wrote to his father the next day, informing him that he did his duty well and often, apparently over eight times according to a note in Burchard's diary. The honeymoon was spent at Blois, and Cesare gave Charlotte many beautiful gifts, which had originally been meant for Carlotta of Aragon. These gifts included jewels as well as gold and silver plate, spoons and ornaments crafted by master goldsmiths in Italy. Charlotte's inventory lists a number of expensive items that were given to her by Cesare.[37]

Yet the couple did not stay together for long at all and "the most content man in the world" began to prepare to join the French attack on Milan. At the end of July, Cesare left his wife behind and joined Louis XII at Lyon to begin the invasion of Italy. He would never see her again.[38]

Taking the Romagna

Louis rode into Milan on 6 October 1499, with Cesare at his side. It had by all accounts been an easy victory, and Ludovico (Il Moro Sforza) had fled his city in September. In fact, as Louis made his way towards Milan, taking over the various duchies, the lords joined up with him with no qualms, just as they had when Charles VIII had invaded five years previously. And it was at this point when Pope Alexander VI decided it was time for Cesare to get his hands on his own Italian state in the north of Italy. The Romagna was to be Cesare's, and so Cesare set out to take it.[39] The Romagna, although technically under papal rule was fiercely independent and the various rulers were petty and cruel. And these rulers were also apostolic vicars or lieutenants of the church, which meant they had to pay a yearly sum (known as the census) to the pope. According to Machiavelli:

> *Before those lords who ruled it were driven out by Pope Alexander VI, the Romagna was a nursery of all the worst crimes.*[40]

The announcement made in October sent many of the ruling lords running for protection, and Lucrezia's ex-husband Giovanni fled from Pesaro to Venice looking for help. Alas, Venice was more than happy to give Pesaro to the Borgias if it meant saving Rimini and Faenza. Caterina Sforza, the infamous Tigress of Forli, sent pleas for help to Florence. But Florence remained neutral, not wanting to offend Louis, and abandoned her to her fate.

At this stage, Cesare was just 24 years old, and it was to be his first military experience. He wouldn't be going it alone either. He would command 100 French troops, but he shared the command with other seasoned French captains. He was confident that taking both Forli and Imola would be easy. For one thing, the ruling family of Imola and Forli had made themselves very unpopular for their cruelty, and Cesare knew their citizens weren't likely to lay down their lives to defend them. And their ruler was a woman – Caterina Sforza. She was no ordinary woman – incredibly beautiful and exceptionally courageous, she had more military experience coming from the Sforza family than many of the young men she would face.[41] After the death of Sixtus IV, the uncle of her first husband, she had held the Castel Sant Angelo in the violent days that followed, and would stride the battlements with a steel corslet over her dress. In 1488, when the citizens of Forli threatened to murder her children, it is said she lifted her skirts and cried, "Look, I have the mould to make more!"[42] In times of war, she wore a full suit of armour like that of a man, except for the curved breastplate to accommodate her bosom.

Caterina's position was precarious, as Cesare knew very well. But she was not someone to underestimate. So much so that even before he reached Imola, he had to turn back and ride quickly to Rome having heard that Caterina had attempted to assassinate the pope. Plague had been raging in Forli and Caterina took a cloth that had been wrapped around a plague-ridden corpse for several days.[43] She sent the cloth in a tube containing apparent letters of surrender. Unfortunately, the messenger she deployed was employed by the Vatican also, and he confided the plot to another

servant. Both men were arrested and thrown into the Castel Sant
Angelo, where they were tortured and confessed. Cesare arrived
on 18 November to check on his father and confer for a few days
before riding north again.

Cesare was right in his predictions, taking Imola and Forli
was easy. Caterina's plot amounted to nothing, and her citizens
offered themselves up to Cesare before his troops even began to
make their way into the city of Imola. He took Imola properly on
27 November. On 15 December, he left for Forli, which he entered
on 17 December. Again the citizens yielded. The only problem
left for Cesare after entering Forli was Caterina, who had holed
herself up in the citadel. At Christmas, Cesare made a personal
attempt to draw her out, riding up to the ramparts to speak with
her. She would have none of it, however, and, according to a report
from a Venetian ambassador, tried to trap him by luring him onto
the drawbridge and raising it. A personal war had begun. On
10 January, Cesare set up his siege guns which, it is said, he took
personal charge over, day and night, and by 12 January 1500, a
breach was opened in the wall.[44] Cesare's troops stormed through,
and vicious hand-to-hand fighting ensued. Caterina was seized by
a Swiss constable who was eager to get his hands on the ransom
money. Cesare then rode to the keep and emerged several hours
later with Caterina. She was taken through the town to where
Cesare was lodged. Cesare's plan for her was simple. She was to be
taken to Rome and held as a 'guest' of the Borgia family.

Following Caterina's imprisonment, rumours yet again started
to spread. Many said he abused and raped her, although there are
also reports at the time that mention nothing of any abuse.[45] Other
reports said he kept her in his room, and the two of them had the
'pleasure' of each other. Is this likely? We will never know, but it
cannot be ruled out that he raped her due to his cruel streak.

On 26 January, Cesare headed to Pesaro. As previously noted,
Giovanni Sforza had already fled the castle, but on the way he
received news that Ludovico was marching on the town of Como.
His army was also shaken with the recall of his French troops, and

left with only 1,500 men he had no hope at all of obtaining victory. So he left a small garrison of troops to look after the Romagna and headed to Rome, with Caterina in tow. He was back in Rome in the last week of February and made a triumphant entry with thousands of his men dressed in beautiful livery. Cesare himself simply wore black, with just the gold collar of the Order of St Michael on his cloak.[46] This is the Cesare that came to be famous, the Cesare who dressed in black and reflected his own personality. There was a stark difference in him from when he left Rome eighteen months previously, dressed in brightly coloured silks. The pope was delighted with Cesare and during Cesare's formal papal welcome was unable to contain his joy, hugging his son close. He even greeted Caterina warmly, giving her a comfortable prison in the Belvedere Villa in the Vatican.[47] While in Rome, Cesare's victory in the Romagna was celebrated and on 29 March 1500, he was given the offices of gonfalonier and captain general of the Church. As well as this, when Alexander created new cardinals, it made him enough money to give to Cesare so he could hire condottieri and resume his career in the Romagna.

Cesare stayed in Rome in the summer of 1500, where he took a mistress by the name of Fiammetta de'Michelis. This lady was a rich courtesan who owned three houses in the city and was exceptionally well-educated. During the summer, Cesare took part in feats that amazed the people of Rome, such as taking part in a bullfight, killing seven bulls after fighting them on horseback in the Spanish style.[48] That summer there was also a nasty accident at the Vatican when a storm made a chimney collapse and the roof fall in. Three men died, but the pope was saved by a fallen beam that protected him from the masonry.[49]

Just over two weeks later, Lucrezia's second husband Alfonso was attacked, as he crossed the piazza of St Peter, and badly wounded. He was taken into the Vatican where he was looked after by Lucrezia, and he began to recover slowly. But suspicion settled over the people of Rome, and only one name was on the lips of the people – Cesare Borgia. It was well-known that Cesare's attitude towards his brother-in-law had grown cool, especially since he had returned from France and noticed just how close Alfonso had grown to the Borgia family. Cesare's name was dragged through the mud to such an extent that he is reported to have said, "I did not wound the Duke, but if I had, it would have been no more than he deserved."[50] Both Lucrezia and Sancia, who were nursing Alfonso back to health along with the help of a doctor sent from Naples, also seemed to have had their suspicions – Lucrezia even made sure that Alfonso only ate food that she and Sancia had prepared out of fear that he could be poisoned at any moment.

But on 18 August, Micheletto burst into the room and took hold of Alfonso's uncle and the envoy of Naples, binding their hands. Lucrezia asked what was going on, and Micheletto replied that he was obeying orders, but if she wanted, she could go to the pope and obtain their release. So off she ran, and when she returned with the pope was barred entry to the room, the guard announcing that Alfonso was dead. Micheletto told the story that Alfonso had stood up and collapsed from his head wound, spilling much blood and dying. This was untrue, and Buchard wrote that Alfonso had been strangled by Micheletto.[51]

Following the incident, there was no doubt who had ordered the murder of Alfonso – Micheletto de Corella was Cesare's right-hand man, and he followed his orders to the letter. Cesare, who had noted just how close Alfonso had grown to his family in his absence in France, was not one to let anyone stand in the way of his relationship with his sister in particular. A convenient excuse was thought up for the murder in which Alfonso, Duke of Bisceglie, had attacked Cesare with a crossbow from a window that overlooked the gardens. And, of course, Cesare had to take vengeance on the man who had threatened his life.

It was said afterwards that this murder was ordered by Cesare, for political reasons, to show people that the Borgias now worked with France rather than being allied with Spain. Yet Cesare had no need to show it in such a way – his French marriage, and his use of French soldiers, was more than enough to make it clear just who the Borgia family was allied with. However, Lucrezia was very much in love with Alfonso and Cesare was exceptionally close to his sister, so could he have ordered the murder due to jealousy? This is the most likely explanation, that Cesare saw Alfonso as a threat to himself and his relationship with his sister. Perhaps there were underlying political issues that link into the shifting alliances of the Borgia family, but it is the reports of a jealous Cesare that caught the imagination of envoys at the time. Following this, Cesare became known as the "terrible" Valentino, and he now had a reputation for complete and utter ruthlessness. After the incident, any murder of importance was attributed to Cesare, and the rumour resurfaced that he had killed his own brother.[52]

Completely grief-stricken at the loss of the husband she so dearly loved, Lucrezia took to the castle at Nepi. She spent four quiet months there, mourning her loss. She was so miserable, so lost and broken after her husband's murder, that she signed her letters "La Infelicissima" or "The most unhappy woman". She truly had loved Alfonso with all her heart, with reports making their way back to Rome that since his death she seemed to have aged to at least three times her age.[53] Previous to this moment, Cesare and Lucrezia had been incredibly close as siblings – so much so that rumours of incest abounded amongst their enemies. But could Lucrezia ever truly forgive her brother for committing such a heinous act? There is no way of ever knowing, but what we do know is that just two days after Alfonso's funeral, Cesare went to visit her. A sign of their close relationship, perhaps, or could it have been Cesare trying to excuse his behaviour in killing Alfonso? Again, there is no way of knowing anything other than the fact that the murder had Cesare Borgia's name now interwoven with fear and terror in a way that it had never been before.

Five days after Alfonso's death, Louis XII arrived in Rome. It was time for Cesare to take up his military standard again. And his reputation would precede him, making him one of the most feared military commanders in Italy. Yet he would also prove to be an extremely gifted military leader who used his head in difficult situations. By 1507, however, despite all his gifts upon the battlefield and his excellent strategic mind, Cesare would be dead. But his accomplishments would go down in history.

Figure 6 - Lucrezia Borgia from *The disputation of St Catherine*
Held in the Borgia apartments.
Photo © Samantha Morris, 2016

Figure 7 - Cesare Borgia's sword scabbard,
held in the Victoria and Albert Museum, London
Photo © Samantha Morris, 2016

Downfall and death

It was 1503 when Cesare Borgia started to lose his grip on the power he held as the son of the pope. The reasoning behind this was simple – the death of his father. Without papal patronage, he would no longer hold the power and prestige that had got him to where he was as gonfalonier of the papal armies. Everything started to unravel in the summer of 1503 when, on Saturday 12 August, Pope Alexander VI became seriously unwell after both he and Cesare had spent an evening dining with a fellow cardinal, Alexander was seized with a fever as well as constant vomiting that lasted for the entire night and well into the next day. On the same day his father became unwell, Cesare too was struck down with the same symptoms. Johannes Buchard, the papal master of ceremonies, recorded the incident in detail:

> *On Saturday morning, August 12th, the pope felt unwell and at about three o'clock in the afternoon he became feverish. Fourteen ounces of blood were taken from him three days later and tertiary fever set in.*

Early on August 17th, he was given some medicine, but he worsened and at about six o'clock on the following morning, he made confession to Don Pietro Gamboa, the bishop of Carinola, who then celebrated Mass in His Holiness's presence. After he had made his own communion, he gave the pope the Host as he sat in his bed and then completed the Mass… At the hour of Vespers he was given Extreme Unction by the Bishop of Carinola, and he expired in the presence of the datary, the bishop and the attendants standing by. Don Cesare, who was also unwell at the time, sent Michelotto with a large number of retainers to close all the doors that gave access to the pope's room… At four o'clock in the afternoon they opened the doors and proclaimed that the pope was dead… Throughout the whole of the pope's illness, Don Cesare never visited his father, nor again after his death, whilst His Holiness for his part never once made the slightest reference to Cesare or Lucrezia. [54]

Cesare's illness was certainly the same as the one that afflicted his father. However, he was treated in a much more dramatic fashion. On 15 August, Cesare was reportedly submerged in a large oil jar filled with ice-cold water, which made the skin peel from his body in shock. The next day, likely due to the shock of the ice bath, Cesare was said to be in danger of losing his life. It was also reported by Giustinian that Cesare suffered throughout his illness with strange fits and delusions. Yet despite being so unwell, Cesare still sent reassuring words to his domain in the Romagna.

Pope Alexander died on 18 June 1503, and by this point, Cesare was well on his way to a full recovery. Despite being weak and exhausted, he recovered with just enough time to save himself from complete and utter ruin. Buchard records in his diaries that Cesare sent his right-hand man, Michelotto de Corella, to close off his father's rooms and remove over 200,000 ducats-worth of items.[55] It is almost certain that, despite his actions, Cesare

mourned the loss of his father. After all, they had worked together
to cement the Borgia dynasty into the minds of both their friends
and enemies, had worked hard to secure lasting alliances, and had
proven to be indispensable to each other time and time again. In
fact, they had been working hard in the five years since Cesare
had first taken up his sword to secure his own position before
Alexander should die. Just two months after his father's death,
Cesare spoke to Machiavelli and stated that he had thought about
everything that could happen when his father died. Except for just
one thing, the possibility that when the pope did die that he too
would be at death's door.

Just twenty-four hours after the death of Pope Alexander VI,
a rumour spread like wildfire around Rome that Cesare Borgia
was dying. Despite his relapse, his enemies who waited with baited
breath for the news that Cesare had died, were disappointed.
Cesare was still the strongest man in Rome. While the cardinals
had no troops or money, Cesare had both as well as the fortress of
the Castel Sant Angelo. The College of Cardinals, due to start the
process of voting in a new pontiff, argued that they did not feel
safe enough to vote for their new pope if Cesare and his troops
were still in Rome. Playing for time, Cesare finally reached an
agreement with the consistory. He would leave Rome only on the
condition that the consistory would reconfirm his as gonfalonier
of the papal armies and that his safety was guaranteed, Venice
would not molest his states in the Romagna and the consistory
would write to the cities within the Romagna urging that they
stayed allied to him once a new pope was elected.[56]

Accompanied by his family and baggage, Cesare finally left
Rome on 2 September 1503. Before leaving, he made a secret
agreement with the French in which the French agreed to protect
both him and his family, safeguard his states and help him get
back what he had lost. In return, Cesare was to serve the King
of France against any power that would try and face him and
would place all of his forces at the French king's disposal. By this
point, Cesare Borgia knew that everything was hanging on the

upcoming papal election – if someone unsympathetic to the Borgia cause were elected, then all would be lost. Thankfully, however, the Spanish cardinals in Cesare's employ would prove to be exceptionally useful. The result was that Alexander VI's nephew, Piccolomini, was elected as Pope Pius III. Pius, a decrepit old man who would not last long in office, did not entirely trust Cesare, and while he did issue some briefs in Borgia's favour, the aged pope told Giustinian that he would give Cesare no more chances as he knew the soldier would come to an "evil end".[57] Cesare was not fooled by Pius's outward show of goodwill, however, and he knew, thanks to his insiders at the papal court, that Pius secretly desired his downfall.

In a well-orchestrated move, Cesare returned to Rome on 3 October 1503, much to the disappointment of his enemies. After he had left, it was widely believed that Cesare was dying, and so to see Duke Valentino returning just as confidant and active as he had ever been must have been a huge blow to his dissenters. Just five days later, on 8 October 1503, Cesare Borgia was once more granted the title of gonfalonier of the papal armies, despite Giuliano della Rovere raging, in true della Rovere fashion, at Pius for allowing Cesare's return.

The populace of Rome, particularly those of the nobility who had always been anti-Borgia, did not want Cesare there. As Pope Pius grew unwell, it became clear that Cesare was surrounded by enemies. During October 1503, for instance, Cesare's home in the Borgo was broken into by the Orsini and Borgia was forced to flee to the Castel Sant Angelo for his own safety.[58] Just two days after this incident, on 17 October 1503, Pope Pius died. His reign had been just twenty-three days long. With a clutch of Spanish cardinals at his disposal, this was incredibly timely for Cesare. But desperate as he was to play pope-maker, there was no question of a Spanish or even a French pope. The majority of the cardinals who would be locked within the Sistine Chapel agreed that the next pontiff should be an Italian, and they all knew who it should be. The elected was none other than Giuliano della Rovere, a man who had been the enemy of the Borgia family for years. Just before della Rovere was elected, news of Cesare's flight into the Vatican following the attack on his home had filtered out of Rome and into the Romagna, affecting the resolve of his allies. Such a flight, in their eyes, proved that the one who had taken their cities by force was losing his grip on the power he once had. Thus, Cesare Borgia had to face up to reality. He signed an agreement agreeing that Cesare's cardinals would vote for him in the conclave. In return, Cesare would retain his title of gonfalonier. The votes of the Spanish cardinals paved the way for della Rovere's election, and on 1 November 1503, Giuliano della Rovere became Pope Julius II.

Now, with his greatest enemy in power, Cesare Borgia had become nothing more than a lone guest in a home that he had once ruled. And the enemy that now sat upon the throne of St Peter would play a definitive role in Cesare Borgia's downfall.

Upon Julius's election, Cesare once more made plans to go to the Romagna. As his states began to revolt against him, taking back the control that he had once had became an obsession. But Borgia had lost in confidence. He was no longer as certain of himself as he had been when he had wrenched Forli from Caterina Sforza's hand, and he became prone to fits of hysterical anger. It was, in a way, as if Cesare Borgia knew he was losing his grip. When, on 14 November 1503, Cesare received news that Florence had refused his troops safe conduct through Tuscany, he realised that Pope Julius II was working against him. Borgia's lack of confidence and self-awareness had him misreading his enemy's steps, something he simply would not have done when he was at the height of his power before Alexander VI's death.

Cesare left Rome for Ostia on 19 November, yet the very next day news reached Rome that Faenza had surrendered to the papal armies. A messenger was sent to Borgia, ordering him not to leave, and when Cesare refused, Julius flew into a fit of rage, a fit of rage so large that, on 21 November, a second messenger was sent with the orders to have Cesare arrested. By the 29 November, Cesare was back in Rome and kept under guard in his old apartments

– now the Raphael Rooms within the Vatican. Days later, news arrived in Rome that Michelotto de Corella, Cesare's right-hand man, had been arrested near Arezzo.[59] It was this move that finally shattered Cesare's will to resist, and he was later moved to the Torre Borgia. In a bitter sense of irony, he was imprisoned in the very same room that Alfonso of Aragon had been murdered upon his own orders. However, it was during his stay within the Torre that Cesare began to work on his resolve. His ability to remain calm in such circumstances certainly impressed his jailers. As was to be expected, Cesare's loyal Spanish cardinals began to petition the pope for their master's release. Julius II steadfastly refused, until an agreement was brokered in which Cesare would order the cessation of his castles within the Romagna and the security of his goods. Julius also agreed to allow Cesare to travel to Ostia in the company of one Bernardino Carvajal, Cardinal of Santa Croce.[60]

Upon arrival in Ostia, Borgia was confined even more rigorously. Yet Carvajal released Cesare without permission from the pope, arranging for a ship to take him to Naples. Cesare made it to Naples. However, he was arrested and found himself once more imprisoned on 24 May 1504, where it was repeatedly demanded that he surrender the castle of Forli. Cesare held out for as long as he could until eventually he was pushed into surrendering the castle on 14 August. Once his jailers had what they wanted, Cesare Borgia found himself on a ship bound for Spain. He was to be the prisoner of the Spanish royalty, who believed him wholeheartedly to be the one who murdered his own brother. His prison was the Castle of Chinchilla, located within the Valencian Mountains. It was during his stay there that Cesare attempted to escape, a story that has almost become the stuff of legend. One account says he attacked his guards while being shown landmarks from the walls, while another says he used the age-old knotted-bedsheet method and climbed from the walls. Whichever story is true, Borgia was kept a much closer eye on after his escape attempt failed.[61]

At some point within 1505, although it isn't clear when exactly, Cesare was transferred to La Mota at the Medina del Campo in Castille. Yet again, during his stay here, Cesare attempted escape, only to have his plan work. On 25 October 1505, three men waited beneath the keep and a rope was let down from Cesare's window. Borgia's servant climbed down first, but fell and severely hurt himself. By the time Cesare began to scale his way down the walls of La Mota, the alarm had been sounded and the rope was cut from above. Cesare fell, landing so poorly that he wasn't able to stand afterwards, so he was carried to a waiting horse. There was no time to save his servant, however, who was found by the guards swarming from La Mota and who executed the boy on the spot. With Cesare's unconscious form slung over a horse, the men who had waited beneath the walls rode for Villanon, where Cesare spent the next month recovering from his wounds. Once recovered, Cesare rode for Navarre, where he met with his brother-in-law, King Jean of Navarre, where he would play his part in bringing the infant Charles V to be the recognised ruler of Castille.

Cesare's end came little over a year after his now fabled escape from La Mota. In February 1507, Cesare once more took to the field of battle where he besieged the castle of Larriaga. By the first week of March, Borgia was once more at King Jean's side in the small town of Viana where another siege was being planned. Borgia and the armies of Navarre were within the town when the weather took a turn for the worst. Cesare did not believe that any attack would be made in such conditions, so, in probably one of the biggest mistakes of his life, Cesare withdrew his sentinels back within the town walls. This mistake was the one that the enemy had been waiting for. The alarm within the town was raised, and confusion reigned supreme. Cesare, as any leader would, ordered that his men mount an attack, and he hastily donned a set of light armour. He rode out of the town gates ahead of his soldiers at such a speed that he swiftly outdistanced them, not realising he was alone until the last possible moment. In the woodland area surrounding Viana, three men ambushed Cesare as he rode

forward. As Cesare raised his arm to attack, a man by the name of
Ximenes Garcia speared him with a lance beneath the arm, where
his armour did not protect him. Mortally wounded, Borgia fought
on until he was overcome by his attackers stabbing him from all
sides. With Cesare overpowered, they stripped him of his armour
and left him naked and bleeding. In one small gesture, perhaps
out of pity for the man who was bleeding his last upon the ground
before them, one of the men covered his genitals with a stone.
On 12 March, just three days before the day that Cesare Borgia's
historic hero Julius Caesar was assassinated, Cesare Borgia died at
the age of just 31.[62]

The men who had ended the life of the lone soldier outside
the walls of Viana had no idea they had killed the infamous
Cesare Borgia. It was only when Cesare's young squire was
shown his armour, bursting into tears at the sight of it, that
it was realised who they had killed. The Constable of Navarre,
Luis de Beaumonte, and the man fighting against both King Jean
and Cesare, was furious at the news. He flew into a rage, having
ordered his men that the famous Il Valentino should be captured
alive at all costs. But de Beaumont could do nothing but retreat as
King Jean moved forward – the king carried Cesare's naked body
back into the town of Viana, from where Cesare had ridden just
hours previously.

Cesare Borgia, the feared Duca de Valentinois, was buried in
the small parish church of Santa Maria in Viana, with a simple
inscription carved into his elaborate marble tomb:

> *Here, in a scant piece of earth, lies he whom all the*
> *world feared.*[63]

However, in 1537 the Bishop of Calahorra ordered that the
tomb be destroyed and his remains placed in unconsecrated
ground, on the basis that a man so feared and believed so 'evil'
should not be granted burial in sacred ground. He was thus
consigned to a small, unmarked grave outside the Church entrance.

In 1945, the grave outside of the church was re-opened. Within it was found the incomplete skeleton of a man, the bones of which were examined by two men, one of whom was the Spanish medical doctor and Cesare Borgia aficionado Victoriano Juaristi Sagarzazu. Between them, Sagarzazu and his colleague Dr Santiago Becerra came to the conclusion that: "The general characteristics such as sex, age, height and the stab wound in the left shoulder-blade, made ante-mortem correlate with the circumstances surrounding Cesare Borgia's life and death,[64]" as well as the fact that the body had lain within its grave for at least 200 years. The bones also showed ante-mortem injuries, including some that showed the individual had at one point fallen from a great height. All in all, Sagarzazu and Becerra concluded that there was nothing to say that this wasn't the body of Cesare Borgia and nothing to refute the tradition that the anti-Christ-like figure had indeed been buried in the ground beneath the pavements. Sagarzazu himself worked tirelessly to restitute Cesare Borgia, even going as far as to help design and create a monument to him. Sadly the elaborate marble monument was destroyed during the Spanish Civil War and, during his lifetime, Cesare's bones were not allowed to be buried back within the grounds of Santa Maria in Viana.

It was in 2007 that Cesare was finally allowed to be once more buried in consecrated ground, permission being granted by the Bishop of Pamplona 500 years after Cesare's death just outside the town. Today, his only monument within the church is a plaque on the floor detailing that beneath it lies the remains of Cesare Borgia, captain general of the Church. There is nothing more to commemorate him other than a bust in the gardens outside the church, almost as if even now people wish to believe in the horror stories that have filtered throughout history and do not wish to give this once great military commander anything more than a passing mention in the annals of history.

Cesare and the Great Pox

One of the most well-known facts about Cesare Borgia is that he suffered from syphilis and often went about wearing a mask. It is said that he wore the mask to cover up the disfigurement on his face that came from the disease. He was considered to be the most handsome man of his day, and so it must have been a shock when he started noticing the tell-tale symptoms of the Great Pox making a show of itself on his face. How did Cesare Borgia contract syphilis? How did he cope with it? How did he have it treated? By the time he died in Navarre, was he cured or did it send him mad enough to rush to his death?

The disease itself was first noticed after the French invasion of Naples in 1495 when it began to spread across Europe. In a way, it was as if Naples was the epicentre of the disease. But how was it spread by the invading French? It is thought the disease was spread through Spanish mercenaries serving under Charles VIII, who caught it in the New World and then spread it amongst the citizens of Naples, who then gave it back to the French. The French spread it further and, thus, across Europe. The disease back then was incredibly lethal and led to thousands of people developing it and its deformities, even leading to widespread death.[65]

In 1497, Cesare Borgia was sent to Naples as papal legate. It had been just six weeks since the death of his brother Juan, Duke of Gandia, and he left with a small army of retainers. Small in this sense involves retainers, camp followers and prelates as well as over 700 horses. Cesare Borgia certainly didn't do things by half. They headed to Capua, where the coronation of Federico as King of Naples was to take place on 6 August, but soon after they had arrived, Cesare fell ill. Sancia and Jofre were dispatched from Rome to nurse him back to health and by 11 August he was well enough to crown Federico. The ceremony itself was lavish, but the barons of the Kingdom of Naples failed to show up. It was one of Cesare's jobs to reconcile them with their new king, but that went down the pan rather quickly. In the end, the only people of note at the ceremony were Cesare's brother Jofre and his wife Sancia – the Prince and Princess of Squillace.[66] Following the coronation ceremony, Cesare was determined to enjoy the Kingdom of Naples. Before he left Naples on 22 August, Cesare and his travelling court had almost impoverished the already poor King of Naples. He also brought something else back with him:

> Monsignor of Valencia has returned from the Kingdom after crowning King Federigo and he is too sick of the French disease.[67]

After Cesare had contracted the disease, his physician Gaspare Torella condemned the use of mercury in treating it and prescribed Cesare a course of ointments, potions and sweating in hot baths. This treatment was deemed a success, and Torella published a book in 1497 extolling the virtues of his treatment over that of mercury. Obviously, it wouldn't have made all that much difference, but within a month or so of returning to Rome it would have seemed like the disease had gone, and no doubt Torella thought his ointments and potions had cured him. The first stage of syphilis tends to disappear within ten to ninety days, before re-appearing later as the secondary stage.[68]

By August 1498, Cesare began working towards getting rid of his cardinal's robes. By this point, he was determined to step into his brother's shoes and become a soldier. He took part in bullfights on horseback and practised leaping astride mules and horses in one jump without touching the harness. He was incredibly proud of both his athletic body and his appearance but by now the symptoms of secondary syphilis were starting to show. The rash began to show itself on his face, somewhat disastrously for the handsome young man, who was planning on impressing his intended new wife and the French court with his good looks.

Gian Lucido Cattaneo wrote, "He is well enough in countenance at present, although he has his face blotched beneath the skin as is usual with the great pox."[69]

Cesare was just 23 when the disease made itself known once more. He wasn't to know, when he first contracted it, that it would disappear on its own only to re-appear later on again. It would haunt him until the end of his life, and he must have been worried about the blotches on his face spoiling his marriage prospects. It seems he was so worried he even kept signing his letters as "Cardinal Valentino" as if he couldn't quite bring himself to believe in his secular future and that the disease would mean he wouldn't marry and would end up back in the church. Even Cattaneo mentions this:

> *Nonetheless he signed himself up to the last moment as Cesar, Card. Valentino ... and this perhaps as a precaution if things did not come out as he wished or that perhaps, because of that face of his, spoiled by the French disease, his wife might refuse him.*[70]

Shortly after Cesare arrived in Marseilles in October 1498, he was struck down again with the malady, as was Cardinal Giuliano della Rovere. Both seemed to recover quickly enough, and Cesare's illness didn't stop him from marrying the wealthy heiress Charlotte d'Albret in May 1499.

Many still believe that Cesare spent much of his time hiding his blotched face behind a mask. Most of these descriptions come from contemporaries hostile to the Borgias who always jumped at the chance of discrediting the family. The image we have of Cesare hiding in the mask is completely fictitious based on a description written by Paolo Giovio, in which he said Cesare looked swarthy and was disfigured by the blotches of syphilis.[71] It seems that after the blotches had disappeared, the chances of disfigurement were small and would only have appeared many years later. At the point in which Giovio was describing Cesare as ravaged by the disease, others such as Capello in around 1500 were pointing out that Cesare, at the age of "twenty five is physically most beautiful, he is tall and well made ...", although this same man later goes on to describe Cesare as a sadistic murderer who had his brother killed.[72]

The next mention we have of Cesare's syphilis is in 1504, just after his father's death and after his imprisonment in the Vatican by Pope Julius II. The year previously, just before his father's death, he had fallen ill with the same fever that killed Pope Alexander. It was most likely to be a malarial fever, although many attribute it to either poison or food poisoning. In April 1504, Cesare made his way to Naples, where he was still quite unwell, and Bernardino de Carvajal reported that at Ostia Cesare had been in a lot of pain with the "French disease" and his face was hideously blotched with nasty looking pustules.[73] It should be noted that we know now that fever, and in particularly malarial fever, was used as a treatment and cure for syphilis up until the advent of penicillin. Cesare's nasty illness the previous year would very likely have cured him and the after effects of said fever.[74]

By the time Cesare was killed in Viana in 1507, did he still have syphilis? Some say he did, and it has been suggested that the disease had affected the senses in his brain so much that he had gone mad and so had ridden to his death. It is, however, an unlikely explanation. Cesare contracted syphilis in 1497, and tertiary syphilis can appear at any point from five to twenty years after the first stage manifests itself. He had syphilis for less than ten years, and it is unlikely that in ten years it would have progressed so far as to make him go mad, and indeed in the lead-up to the day of his death, there is no evidence at all that he had gone mad at all. He certainly seemed to be in control of his senses and even in the bleakest moments he never lost hope and always kept his mind on the prize. He was a reckless man certainly, and the way he rode to his death on his own is very similar to a description made of him in 1503, when he rode at a group of Orsinis (again, completely on his own), saying he would rather die in the saddle than in his bed. And, as mentioned previously, it's very likely that he didn't even have the disease thanks to the dangerous fever he suffered from in 1503.

We must remember, though, that after more than 500 years, it is almost impossible to say whether he died as a result of syphilis affecting his brain or whether he did indeed still have it at the time of his death. All we can say is that he had it at one point and that it certainly affected his life in many ways although, like many things with Cesare's story, most of what we think about his illness today comes from anti-Borgia propaganda Did he hide his ravaged face behind a mask? Probably not. Did he wear a mask? Yes, but it was more likely to keep himself disguised so he wouldn't be noticed, not to hide a blotched face away. The blotches would have disappeared anyway, and physical disfigurement in such a short space of time was highly unlikely. But, like the incest tales, it's another of these stories that many seem determined to hold on to. But why? Because it makes the man come across as more monstrous than he ever truly was.

The legend and legacy of the Borgia family

The legend of the Borgia family, and in particular the legend of Cesare Borgia, has sprung up from the pages of history. It is ever lurking amongst the historical fact, desperately trying to seep on through into public consciousness. But it is the legend that has captured people's imaginations leading to a plethora of historical fiction novels, television shows and even an opera. It is these stories that draw on the rumours grasped at by the enemies of the Borgias back during the Renaissance, dramatising the propaganda and making the family seem much more corrupt and evil than they truly were. The same thing happened time and time again, from the moment of Alexander's death, the image of the Borgias as poisoning, incestuous and corrupt individuals becoming ingrained in the imagination of people for centuries.

The idea of the Borgia family as evil stems mainly from Protestant propagandists in the sixteenth and seventeenth centuries, wishing to sully the name of the Catholic Church following the influx of reformist ideals. The same ideas of pacts with the devil are repeated time and again. For instance, in 1611 Phillipe de Mournay wrote:

> *Some recount Alexander's pact with the devil. The Devil's working in Alexander's actions is clear. All agree that no one ever reached the Papacy by more evil arts.*

In fact the idea of the Borgias, Alexander, in particular, making pacts with the devil is something that is seen time and again. Alexander even has a part to play in the legends of Faust. According to the legend, Faust first saw Rodrigo Borgia calling on the devil while studying at Bologna, and, in return, the devil offered Borgia the papal crown.[75]

While myths and legends abound about Rodrigo Borgia and his links to the devil, there is so much more written about the legend and legacy of Cesare Borgia himself. Alongside the spurious rumours that erupted during Cesare's life, one of the first instances being put into book form was in 1655, when Tomaso Tomasi wrote the influential *Vita del Duca Valentino*. What is particularly interesting about the *Vita* is that Tomasi states it is Cesare's mother who led him towards becoming the evil tyrant. And in a later version, added to in the 1670s by Gregorio Leti, Cesare is spoken of as a man with ferocious bloodlust, even going so far as to link Cesare's actions in life to demonic possession.[76] One work written before Tomasi's, which truly cemented the legend of Cesare's evilness, was *Elogia*, written by Paolo Giovio, Bishop of Nocera, in 1551. Giovio stated that Cesare Borgia was "born of accursed seed", had murdered his brother and, as one of the worst tyrants history had ever seen, was the "plague of an unhappy age".[77] It is interesting to note how yet again the idea of being accursed and evil is mentioned – an ever occurring theme in the legend that has built up around Cesare and his family.

Cesare Borgia has had champions, however, and there is one in particular that has stuck in the mind of many. But, Niccolo

Machiavelli's support of Cesare, rather than helping to show that Cesare was not a tyrant, actually damaged his name almost irrevocably. The most well-known of Machiavelli's works that praises Cesare Borgia is the infamous *Il Principe*, a book that praised the methods in which Cesare unified the Romagna and stated that the cruelties he inflicted were a method that all princes should adopt to unify their people. The book was incredibly popular and even had an essay written on it, by a French Protestant by the name of Innocent Gentillet, which was translated into multiple languages and reprinted in twenty-four editions. What is particularly interesting here is that, yet again, the devil and evil magic are mentioned and that Cesare's vices should not be extolled as any virtue as God would punished them. According to Gentillet, Cesare's death was a completely just punishment by God. Even English authors at the time of Charles stated that Borgia was evil and his downfall completely just. In *A Mirror for Princes*, Machiavelli was spoken of as the man who groomed Cesare and twisted him into a puppet to be used as a perfect example of virtue. The author and preacher William Struther stated wholeheartedly that Borgia, who had begun his reign of terror "with the killing of his elder brother", was made an example of by God for daring to rule his states with contempt of God and by utter fear.[78] It is certainly unlikely that Machiavelli acted as a master of the Borgia, rather, Machiavelli admired Cesare Borgia's methods, seeing him as a key player in the politics of his time, and he saw that his methods worked. On the subject of tyranny, Edward, Earl of Clarendon, in his *History of the Rebellion*, states that Oliver Cromwell is the next Cesare Borgia, a royalist propaganda piece to show that Cromwell was as much of a tyrant as the legendary Cesare Borgia, who had achieved his aims through cunning and cruel acts.[79] Cromwell had brought down a king through war and began a reign of tyranny within England. To the seventeenth-century mind, therefore, Oliver Cromwell and Cesare Borgia were one and the same.

There are, of course, other methods in which the legend of Cesare Borgia has remained in the public imagination. Other than biographies written by those in the past with a political or religious agenda we have plays and operas based on the legend of the evil family, which in turn has led to, in the modern era, historical novels and television dramas. One of the first plays to star the Borgia family was Barnabe Barnes' *The Divil's Charter*, which was performed at the court of King James I of England in 1607. Just two years previously, King James had been the target of a 'popish' plot, in which Guy Fawkes and a group of conspirators planned on blowing up the Houses of Parliament. So is it any wonder that King James was attracted to a play that centres around a pope who had gained his crown by hatching a plot with Satan? The play itself is not only anti-papal but anti-Machiavellian as well. After all, Barnes attacked Machiavelli by name in his 1606 work, *Foure books of Offices*.[80] Another play that concerns itself deeply with anti-Catholic ideals as well as the idea of Cesare Borgia being evil incarnate is Nathaniel Lee's *Caesar Borgia*, published in 1680. At this point, England was once more undergoing a time of intense anti-papal feeling, with the only heir to the throne being the Catholic James, Duke of York. Lee's play deals with the extensive use of poisoning and even starts with a prologue by Dryden, in which he states that poisoning is the way of things there, and the devil gives thanks for it.[81]

Of the modern day dramatisations, both in the written word and on screen, we see a sexed-up version of an already notorious family that draws on the rumours of murder, incest and political backstabbing, twisting them into stories that the public wants to believe is historical fact. The stories of incest between Cesare and his sister are particularly prevalent in these mediums. For instance, in Jean Kalogridis' *The Borgia Bride*, incest and sexual intrigue are the main plot points. Comparing this to television, Showtime's *The Borgias*, starring Francois Arnaud as Cesare Borgia and Holliday Grainger as Lucrezia Borgia, shows the siblings sleeping together on Lucrezia's wedding night. Conversely, the Canal + *Borgia Faith and Fear* does not cross that line, rather showing that the siblings walked a very fine line that could so very easily have been crossed on many occasions.

When comparing the modern day television shows, there are some huge differences between the two, and one of them has become ingrained within the public mindset with the belief that events shown are indeed historical fact. Showtime's *The Borgias*, to those who don't know the Renaissance era, is a good solid piece of entertainment with its high budget, lavish costumes and an all-star cast. But if you look beyond the veil of beautiful sets and incredible acting, there are some glaring historical errors, and not all of them are based on Cesare himself. For instance, the show often shows a view of the dome of St Peter's. This did not exist at the time of the Borgias. Rather, the first plans came into existence in 1506, and the dome wasn't completed until 1590. Glossing over this, however, *The Borgias* also showed Cesare stabbing his brother and throwing his body into the Tiber, Lucrezia Borgia resorting to poisoning, and the death of Lucrezia's second husband at the hands of both Cesare and his sister. Add this to the incestuous overtures of the show and you have a drama that has sprung from the rumour and propaganda that swept Rome at the time of the Borgia family. On the other hand, Canal +'s version, *Faith and Fear*, is much more historically accurate. The Vatican is modelled on the old St Peter's Basilica and you clearly see Cesare's transformation from cardinal to soldier. In this version, Cesare, played by Mark Ryder, and Lucrezia, played by Isolda Dychauk, never cross the line and sleep together. It is clear the siblings were close, perhaps closer than we in this age believe that siblings should be, and the series clearly shows how the rumours of incest began. Cesare even says in the final episode of season 1: "The whole world believes we are lovers. Perhaps we should prove them right." But before any lines can be crossed, the two are interrupted by Lucrezia's lover, Perotto, who is hiding behind the curtains.

Faith and Fear remains true to the history of Cesare Borgia in many ways. Throughout the three seasons, Cesare truly becomes

HISTORY "In a Nutshell" SERIES

the warlord that history says he was. Juan's death was orchestrated by an unknown assailant rather than his own brother, and the Siege of Forli, unlike in *The Borgias*, was done correctly. Although there were some historical inaccuracies, as is to be expected in any historical drama, *Faith and Fear* draws on historical fact rather than latching onto rumours and twisting them to sex-up a script. It must be said, though, that *The Borgias* was far more popular than *Faith and Fear*. This is simply because the general public prefers a sexed-up version of history. The stories shown in the Showtime version are a twisted account of history, based solely on rumour and propaganda.

But now, as throughout history, people love a good gossip. They want stories of political intrigue and forbidden love, stories that both disgust them and draw them in. It is because of this that modern day adaptations of the Borgia history draw on the rumours that sparked during the Renaissance and use them to their advantage. Despite the fact that these rumours are simply just that, rumours, they do make for some spectacular viewing both on the pages of novels and on television.

Would Cesare Borgia approve of the fact that his name has lived on in such a way? Today, despite the efforts of historians, he is still seen as an evil man who slept with his sister. It is forgotten that he unified the Romagna, albeit using some cruel acts, and that under his rule the cities he took over prospered. The behaviour that both he and his family exhibited was completely normal, they were people of their time. Murder and political intrigue were things in which every single noble family took part. Due to the fact that the Borgia family were in a position of power, the fact that they were Spaniards, these behaviours were taken and twisted into something more simply to show them as evil.

Unfortunately for them, despite the efforts of many to rehabilitate them, and thanks to the continued vilification through the public medium of books, plays and television, the idea of the Borgia family being the most evil family in history will never truly go away.

Epilogue

After Cesare's death in Viana, there were still members of his family living that were greatly affected by his loss. Indeed, his death echoed through the years and affected not only his direct family but his descendants as well. The three who were most affected were, of course, his wife, Charlotte, and his daughter, Louise, as well as his sister Lucrezia. These three women shared something with Cesare that many did not – a closeness and genuine love, despite the fact that Charlotte never saw her husband after he left France and Louise never even met her father. Nevertheless, there was the close bond of blood between Cesare and the women and, as such, his death affected them all the most.

Although we don't know how or where exactly Charlotte d'Albret received the news of her husband's death, it can easily be imagined just how heartbroken she was. After all, in the years of their separation she had wholeheartedly believed her husband would come back to her. Her letters clearly showed how much she believed he would return, and it can be deduced with certainty just how much she loved him in the way she mourned him. For the remainder of her life, she dressed entirely in black, swathed her home in black and even had her daughter's little pony given black trappings. Charlotte d'Albret outlived her husband by just six years, and never once did she ease up on the period of mourning that she forced upon her daughter and household.

Despite the love that the originally uncertain bride apparently bore for her husband, during their years of separation she never once tried to reach out to see her husband. In 1503, every effort was made to convince Charlotte to go to Italy. Cesare himself even sent a messenger to her; King Louis tried to reason with her, but she steadfastly refused to go after hearing of his cruelty in the Romagna. Louise, Cesare and Charlotte's daughter, was even used as a pawn in a method of getting Charlotte to Italy. In 1503, Cesare was said to have entered talks with Guiliano della Rovere to have their children betrothed to one another, an act that King Louis of France also tried to use to his advantage in the matter.[82] But Louis' threats to send Louise to her father and Cesare's talks towards a della Rovere marriage fell through, and still Charlotte refused to go to her husband. Instead, she loved her husband from a distance, seeming to cling to the image of the man she had known for just a short while after their marriage rather than admitting to the cruel reality of who Cesare Borgia truly was.

Louise Borgia's childhood was spent away from her father – she never once met the man, and was only seven years old when he was killed in Viana. But up until her death at the age of 53 in 1553, she signed her letters as "Louise De Valentinois" and made sure she used the titles she inherited from her father. After all, those titles had been torn away from her father during his lifetime thanks to the actions of King Louis XII. In 1507, Louis declared that Cesare had forfeited all rights to the title of Lord of Issouden thanks to "his treachery toward his former ally during the wars in Italy".[83] This treachery involved such actions as his threatening Florence, despite it being under the protection of France, and his driving the Bentivoglio family out of Bologna, despite Louis' explicit orders for that not to happen. King Louis believed he was right in tearing Cesare's titles away from him for this, yet he also pulled Charlotte d'Albret into it and, thus, it affected Louise as well.

Louise married twice. At the age of seventeen she was married to a French widower, Louis de la Tremouille, Lord of Thouars. Louis was killed fighting for King Francis I at the Battle of Pavia in 1525, leaving Louise a widow. Five years after her first husband's death, she married Phillipe de Bourbon-Busset, a member of the illegitimate branch of the Bourbon family. With Phillipe, Louise had six children. Through them, Cesare Borgia's direct descendants still exist today. There is only one recorded description of Louise Borgia, written by the biographer of Anne of Brittany, in which she is described as "chaste, virtuous and gentle as her father was possessed, cruel and wicked".[84] Perhaps not the greatest description of Cesare, but it serves its purpose in describing Louise. As the only legitimate child of Cesare Borgia, it would have been important for Louise not to be tarred with the same brush.

Following Cesare's death, the squire, who had been with Cesare at the time, took the news to Ferrara, where it was given to Lucrezia. Ippolito d'Este was reportedly too worried to give Lucrezia the news, and so the task was given to a friar by the name of Raffaelo. The news of her beloved brother's death understandably broke Lucrezia's heart. After all, she had lost so much, and she was reported to have cried out that: "The more I try to follow God's will, the more he visits me with sorrows."[85] She shut herself away in her chambers, crying her brother's name and refusing to leave her bed. But in public, she remained calm and had a remarkable self-control just as she had done after the murder of her second husband. Lucrezia had few with whom to share her grief properly and, in her grief, she turned to the two main men still in her life – her husband, Alfonso, and her lover Francesco Gonzaga. However, in the months following her brother's death, Lucrezia only wrote to her husband. She did not send letters to Gonzaga.

Lucrezia passed away in 1519 at the age of 39, after giving birth to a girl. After the birth, Lucrezia fell into a grave illness likely due to the accumulation of menstrual blood within her womb during pregnancy, and the doctors tried everything, even down to cutting off her hair. But her life could not be saved. She was buried in the convent of Corpus Domini in Ferrara, a grave she now shares with her husband and two of her children, including little Isabella, the child she'd just given birth to when she died and who survived her mother by just two years.

There is one member of Cesare's family who went a long way to get rid of the stigma of the Borgia name, at least in his own time. His name was Francis, grandson of Cesare's brother Juan, who had died in suspicious circumstances in 1497. And he was the only member of the Borgia family made a saint.

Francis was born in 1510 in Gandia, Spain, and after the death of his wife in 1546, he decided to join the Society of Jesus, or Jesuits. Eventually, in 1565, he was elected as general of the Jesuit society. Francis led an incredibly humble life and had remarkable success in his life as a Jesuit. He founded colleges as well as advising kings and popes. Throughout his life, Francis steadfastly refused to have a portrait of himself painted, and it was only when he was dying that his fellow brothers managed to get an artist into the same room as him. They sneaked an artist in as he slept, but only a basic sketch was made before Francis made a gesture that he did not want it to carry on, and rolled over to hide his face. As night fell on 30 September 1572, one of his brothers tried to get Francis to drink some soup, and the dying man managed only a mouthful. He died at a little after midnight on 1 October 1572, and according to Brother Marco, Francis "died as he had lived, with marvellous peace and serenity".[86] Francis was canonised in 1671 by Pope Clement XI for his pious life and great work for the Jesuit society.

Cesare's descendants still exist today, mainly through the children of his daughter, as well as those of Saint Francis Borgia. But what also exists is an idea of the House of Borgia being fantastically wicked and corrupt, rife with sexual intrigue and corruption. Despite the good works of his sister and his brother's grandson, the stories that come simply from anti-Borgia propaganda are what have remained firmly within the public imagination. But as we have seen, rather than being an evil man, Cesare Borgia was simply a man of his time. While he committed cruelties and atrocities that were normal during times of war, Cesare Borgia was also an incredibly intelligent man, an able politician and a talent upon the battlefield. He was also a man whose life centred around his family. He was incredibly close to his sister, so much so that it led to accusations of incest, and worked side-by-side with his father until the moment his father died.

Whether or not Cesare Borgia was guilty of many of the accusations of incest and corruption levelled against him throughout the years, there is one thing we can say for certain. Cesare Borgia is a man who excites the imagination of historians, writers and the television-watching public. His is a name that will never truly go away, and a name that has become legend.

Figure 8 - The tomb marble of Cesare Borgia
at Iglesia Santa Maria de la Asunción Viana
Photo © Peter Schulze

Bibliography

Bradford, Sarah (1976) *Cesare Borgia: His Life and Times,* Macmillan.

Bradford, Sarah (2005) *Lucrezia Borgia: Life, Love and Death in Renaissance Italy,* Penguin.

trans. Bull, George (2003) *The Prince* by Niccolo Machiavelli, Longman.

Cruz, Salvador Martin (2007) *Victoriano Juaristi Sagarzazu (1880-1949) El Ansia De Saber. Datos Para Una Biografia,* Gobierno de Navarra.

Durant, Will (1953) *The Renaissance,* Simon and Schuster.

Early Books On Syphilis in The British Medical Journal, Vol. 1, No. 3463, May 21, 1927.

Hibbert, Christopher (2009) *The Borgias And Their Enemies,* Houghton Mifflin.

Hilgarth, J. N. (1996) *The Image Of Alexander VI and Cesare Borgia in The Sixteenth and Seventeenth Centuries* in Journal Of The Warburg and Courtauld Institutres, Vol. 59: 119-129.

Hollingsworth, Mary (2011) *The Borgias: History's Most Notorious Dynasty,* Quercus.

Lee, Nathaniel (1680) *Caesar Borgia: Son Of Pope Alexander the Sixth, a Tragedy, in five acts and in verse*

Lev, Elizabeth (2011), *The Tigress Of Forli*, Houghlin Mifflin Harcourt.

Machiavelli, Niccolo (1883) *Discourses On The First Decade of Titus Livus Vol 3 Chapter XXIX,* Kegan Paul, Trench & Co.

ed. McCray, W. D. (1888) *Clarendon's History Of The Rebellion Vol IV* by Edward Hyde, Earl of Clarendon, Clarendon Press.

McKerrow, R. B. (1904) *The Devil's Charter by Barnabe Barnes, edited from the Quarto of 1607,* A. Uystpruyst.

Miron, E. L. (1911) *Duchess Derelict: Charlotte d'Albret Duchess of Valentinois,* S. Paul & Co.

Norwich, John Julius (2012) *The Popes: A History,* Vintage.

Oppenheimer, Paul (2011) *Machiavelli: A Life Beyond Ideology,* Continuum.

trans. Parker, Geoffrey (1963) *At The Court Of The Borgia* by Johann Burchard, Folio Society.

Strathern, Paul (2010) *The Artist, The Philosopher and The Warrior,* Vintage.

Struther, William (1632) *A Looking Glass For Princes and People*

trans. Thurmel, Joseph (1923) *Le Journal de Jean Burchard,* Les Editions Reider.

Tomasi, Tomaso (1671) *La Vita Di Cesare Borgia, Detto Poi Il Duca Valentino*

Yeo, Margaret (1936) *The Greatest of The Borgias,* Bruce Publishing Co.

Endnotes

1.   Norwich, *The Popes*, p214
2.   Bradford, *Cesare Borgia His Life and Times*, p 13
3.   Hibbert, *The Borgias and their Enemies*, p12-14
4.   Hollingsworth, *The Borgias: History's Most Notorious Dynasty*, p123; Sarah Bradford, *Cesare Borgia His Life and Times*, p17.
5.   Hollingsworth, p123
6.   Bradford, *Cesare Borgia His Life and Times*, p19
7.   Bradford, *Lucrezia Borgia: Life, Love and Death in Renaissance Italy*, p15; Bradford, *Cesare Borgia His Life and Times*, p19
8.   Bradford, *Cesare Borgia His Life and Times*, p21
9.   Ibid., p23
10. Ibid., p26
11. Ibid., p27; Norwich, *The Popes*, p251
12. Bradford, *Cesare Borgia His Life and Times*, p30-31
13. Ibid., p35; Strathern, *The Artist, the Philosopher and the Warrior*, p 68
14. Ibid., p68-69
15. Bradford, *Cesare Borgia His Life and Times*, p41
16. Strathern, *The Artist, the Philosopher and the Warrior*, p70; Bradford, *Cesare Borgia His Life and Times*, p41
17. Strathern, p 73; Bradford, *Cesare Borgia His Life and Times*, p49; Hibbert, *The Borgias and their Enemies*, p77
18. Hollingsworth, *The Borgias*, p213
19. Bradford, *Cesare Borgia His Life and Times*, p59
20. Burchard, *At The Court Of The Borgia*, p135, Durant, *The Renaissance*, p411

21. Bradford, *Cesare Borgia His Life & Times*, p61
22. Ibid., p63
23. Hibbert, *The Borgias and their Enemies*, p110
24. Burchard, *Le Journal de Jean Burchard*, p292
25. Burchard, *At The Court Of The Borgia*, p 67
26. Bradford, *Cesare Borgia His Life and Times*, p64
27. Ibid., p65-66; Hollingsworth, *The Borgias*, p223
28. Bradford, *Cesare Borgia His Life and Times*, p71
29. Strathern, *The Artist, the Philosopher and the Warrior*, p82; Hibbert, *The Borgias and their Enemies*, p114
30. Bradford, *Cesare Borgia His Life and Times*, p71; Bradford, *Lucrezia Borgia: Life, Love and Death in Renaissance Italy*, p67-8; Hibbert, *The Borgias and their Enemies*, p118
31. Bradford, *Cesare Borgia His Life and Times*, p77
32. Ibid., p81; Hibbert, *The Borgias and their Enemies*, p125; Hollingsworth, *The Borgias: History's Most Notorious Dynasty*, p253.
33. Hibbert, *The Borgias and their Enemies*, p130; Strathern, *The Artist, the Philosopher and the Warrior*, p81; Bradford, *Cesare Borgia His Life and Times*, p84.
34. Strathern, *The Artist, the Philosopher and the Warrior*, p82; Hibbert, *The Borgias and their Enemies*, p134.
35. Hibbert, *The Borgias and their Enemies*, p136
36. Bradford, *Cesare Borgia His Life and Times*, p99.
37. Miron, *Duchess Derelict: Charlotte D'Albret Duchess of Valentinois*, p157
38. Ibid., p102; Strathern, *The Artist, the Philosopher and the Warrior*, p83.
39. Bradford, *Cesare Borgia His Life and Times*, p105
40. Machiavelli, *Discourses*, p263
41. Strathern, *The Artist The Philosopher and The Warrior*, p86
42. Lev, *The Tigress of Forli*, p133
43. Bradford, *Cesare Borgia His Life and Times*, p110
44. Lev, *The Tigress of Forli*, p225
45. Ibid., p230
46. Bradford, *Cesare Borgia His Life and Times*, p114
47. Lev, *The Tigress of Forli*, p235
48. Bradford, *Cesare Borgia His Life and Times*, p121-122
49. Hibbert, *The Borgias and Their Enemies*, p161
50. Bradford, *Lucrezia Borgia: Life, Love and Death in Renaissance Italy*, p90
51. Ibid., p91
52. Ibid., p93; Burchard, *At The Court Of The Borgia*, p183
53. Hibbert, *The Borgias and Their Enemies*, p165
54. Parker/Burchard, *At The Court Of The Borgia*, p220.
55. Ibid., p221
56. Bradford, *Lucrezia Borgia: Life Love and Death in Renaissance Italy*, p202; Hollingsworth, *The Borgias: History's Most Notorious Dynasty*, p317.
57. Strathern, *The Artist The Philosopher and The Warrior*, p267-268.
58. Bradford, *Cesare Borgia His Life and Times*, p245

59. Bradford, *Lucrezia Borgia: Life Love and Death in Renaissance Italy*, p211
60. Strathern, *The Artist, The Philosopher and The Warrior*, p336.
61. Bradford, *Cesare Borgia: His Life and Times*, p274
62. Ibid., p286-287; Bradford, *Lucrezia Borgia: Life Love and Death in Renaissance Italy*, p270; Strathern, *The Artist, The Philosopher and the Warrior*, p368; Hollingsworth, *The Borgias: History's Most Notorious Dynasty*, p337; Oppenheimer, *Machiavelli: A Life Beyond Ideology*, p197-198.
63. Bradford, *Cesare Borgia His Life and Times*, p288
64. Salvador Martin Cruz, *Victoriano Juaristi Sagarzazu*, p187-188
65. Hibbert, *The Borgias and Their Enemies*, p79
66. Bradford, *Cesare Borgia His Life and Times*, p67
67. Ibid., p68
68. *Early Books on Syphilis*, p927
69. Hibbert, *The Borgias and Their Enemies*, p125
70. Bradford, *Cesare Borgia His Life and Times*, p84
71. Strathern, *The Artist The Philosopher and the Warrior*, p 215
72. Bradford, *Cesare Borgia His Life and Times*, p130
73. Ibid., p265
74. Ibid., p291
75. Hilgarth, The Image of Alexander VI and Cesare Borgia in the Sixteenth and Seventeenth Centuries, p121.
76. Tomasi, *La Vita Di Cesare Borgia, Detto Poi Il Duca Valentinto*, p168
77. Paolo Giovio, *Elogia Virorum Illustrium* (Rome 1972), p378 mentioned in Hilgarth, The Image of Alexander VI and Cesare Borgia in the Sixteenth and Seventeenth Centuries, p119-129.
78. Struther, *A Looking Glass for Princes and People*, p93-94
79. McCray, *Clarendon's History of the Rebellion Vol. IV*, p304-305
80. McKerrow, *The Devil's Charter by Barnabe Barnes* – The entire play runs on the ideals of anti Papal and anti Machiavellian plot points.
81. Lee, *Caesar Borgia: Son of Pope Alexander the Sixth, a Tragedy, in five acts and in verse*
82. Miron, *Duchess Derelict: Charlotte d'Albret Duchess Of Valentinois*, p311
83. Ibid., p287
84. Bradford, *Cesare Borgia His Life and Times*, p295
85. Bradford, *Lucrezia Borgia Life, Love and Death in Renaissance Italy*, p363-366
86. Yeo, *The Greatest Of The Borgias*, p309-311

Illustrations

Meet Samantha Morris

Samantha studied archaeology at the University of Winchester where her interest in the history of the Italian Renaissance began. Since graduating University, her interest in the Borgia family has grown to such an extent that she is always looking for new information on the subject as well as fighting against the age-old rumours that haunt them. Samantha describes herself as an accountant by day, historian and author by night.

Her first published book is *Cesare Borgia in a Nutshell*, a brief biography which aims to dispel the myths surrounding a key member of the Borgia family. She runs the popular Borgia website *https://theborgiabull.com/* and would love to "see" you on her site.

Other books in this series:

Mary Boleyn

in a nutshell

History "In a Nutshell" Series

SARAH BRYSON

ISBN: 978-84-943721-1-7

In **Mary Boleyn in a Nutshell, Sarah Bryson** discusses the controversies surrounding Mary Boleyn's birth, her alleged relationships with two kings, her portraiture and appearance, and her life and death. Mary survived the brutal events of 1536 and was able to make her own choices, defying the social rules of her times by marrying for love. It is from Mary that the Boleyn bloodline extends to the present day.

Thomas Cranmer
in a nutshell

History
"In a Nutshell"
Series

BETH VON STAATS

ISBN: 978-84-943721-3-1

In **Thomas Cranmer in a Nutshell**, **Beth von Staats** discusses the fascinating life of **Thomas Cranmer**, from his early education, through his appointment to Archbishop of Canterbury, his growth in confidence as a reformer, the writing of two versions of the English Book of Common Prayer and eventually to his imprisonment, recantations and execution.

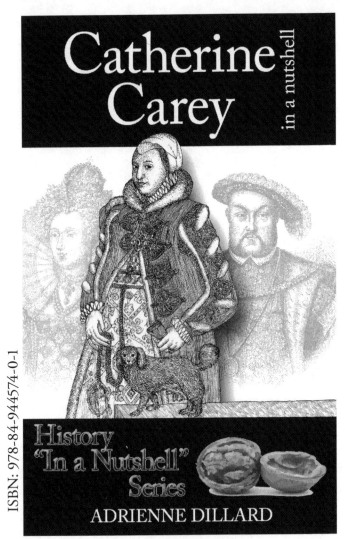

Catherine Carey

in a nutshell

History "In a Nutshell" Series

ADRIENNE DILLARD

ISBN: 978-84-944574-0-1

Catherine Carey in a Nutshell examines the life of Catherine Carey, daughter of Mary Boleyn, from the controversy surrounding her paternity through her service to Henry VIII's queens, the trials of life in Protestant exile during the Tudor era, and the triumphant return of the Knollys family to the glittering court of the Virgin Queen. This book brings together what is known about one of Queen Elizabeth I's most trusted and devoted ladies for the first time in one concise, easy-to-read book.

Sweating Sickness

in a nutshell

History "In a Nutshell" Series

CLAIRE RIDGWAY

ISBN: 978-15-009962-2-2

In **Sweating Sickness in a Nutshell**, **Claire Ridgway** examines what the historical sources say about the five epidemics of the mystery disease which hit England between 1485 and 1551, and considers the symptoms, who it affected, the treatments, theories regarding its cause and why it only affected English people.

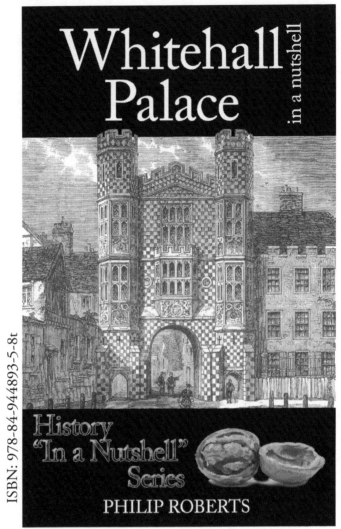

Whitehall Palace

in a nutshell

History "In a Nutshell" Series

PHILIP ROBERTS

ISBN: 978-84-944893-5-8t

In **Whitehall Palace in a Nutshell**, researcher and author *Philip Roberts* delves into the history of England's most important and significant lost building, a palace which had 2000 rooms and covered 23 acres in its heyday.

Using his unprecedented connections, Philip has been able to gain access to the historical places in Whitehall Palace which still exist today, many of which are not open to public access.

Philip Roberts, a member of the Mary Rose Trust Information Group Team for well over 20 years, has a passion for Tudor re-enactment and educating people about history.

Edward VI
in a nutshell

ISBN: 978-84-945937-0-3

History
"In a Nutshell"
Series

KYRA KRAMER

Born twenty-seven years into his father's reign, Henry's VIII's son, Edward VI, was the answer to a whole country's prayers. Precocious and well-loved, his life should have been idyllic and his own reign long and powerful. Unfortunately for him and for England, that was not to be the case. Crowned King of England at nine years old, Edward was thrust into a world of power players, some who were content to remain behind the throne, and some who would do anything to control it completely. Devoutly Protestant and in possession of an uncanny understanding of his realm, Edward's actions had lasting effects on the religious nature of the kingdom and would surely have triggered even more drastic changes if he hadn't tragically and unexpectedly died at the age of fifteen.

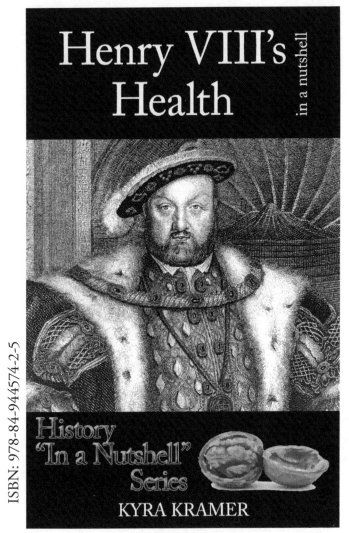

Henry VIII's Health

in a nutshell

ISBN: 978-84-944574-2-5

History "In a Nutshell" Series

KYRA KRAMER

Tudor histories are rife with "facts" about Henry VIII's life and health, but as a medical anthropologist, Kyra Kramer, author of Blood Will Tell, has learned one should never take those "facts" at face value. In Henry VIII's Health in a Nutshell, Kramer highlights the various health issues that Henry suffered throughout his life and proposes a few new theories for their causes, based on modern medical findings.

Known for her readability and excellent grasp of the intricacies of modern medical diagnostics, Kyra Kramer gives the reader a new understanding of Henry VIII's health difficulties, and provides new insights into their possible causes.

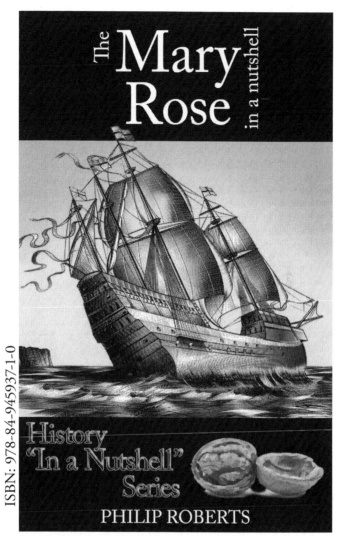

The Mary
Rose

in a nutshell

ISBN: 978-84-945937-1-0

History
"In a Nutshell"
Series

PHILIP ROBERTS

Henry VIII's prized flagship sank in 1545 under the watchful eye of the king himself. With it, over 500 men tragically lost their lives.

The Mary Rose in a Nutshell takes us up-to-date with the theories and finds from this, the only Tudor ship in the world. From her construction in 1511, through expansion and refitting, to the Battle of the Solent, and then on to various attempts at salvage, the story of the Mary Rose is amazing. 437 years after she sank, her hull was brought back to the surface and an intense conservation effort was begun.

HISTORY IN A NUTSHELL SERIES

Sweating Sickness - **Claire Ridgway**
Mary Boleyn - **Sarah Bryson**
Thomas Cranmer - **Beth von Staats**
Henry VIII's Health - **Kyra Kramer**

Catherine Carey - **Adrienne Dillard**
The Pyramids - **Charlotte Booth**
The Mary Rose - **Philip Roberts**
Whitehall Palace - **Philip Roberts**

NON FICTION HISTORY

Anne Boleyn's Letter from the Tower - **Sandra Vasoli**
Jasper Tudor - **Debra Bayani**
Tudor Places of Great Britain - **Claire Ridgway**
Illustrated Kings and Queens of England - **Claire Ridgway**
A History of the English Monarchy - **Gareth Russell**
The Fall of Anne Boleyn - **Claire Ridgway**
George Boleyn: Tudor Poet, Courtier & Diplomat - **Ridgway & Cherry**
The Anne Boleyn Collection - **Claire Ridgway**
The Anne Boleyn Collection II - **Claire Ridgway**
Two Gentleman Poets at the Court of Henry VIII - **Edmond Bapst**
A Mountain Road - **Douglas Weddell Thompson**

HISTORICAL FICTION

The Devil's Chalice - **D.K.Wilson**
Falling Pomegranate Seeds - **Wendy J. Dunn**
Struck with the Dart of Love: Je Anne Boleyn 1 - **Sandra Vasoli**
Truth Endures: Je Anne Boleyn 2 - **Sandra Vasoli**
The Colour of Poison - **Toni Mount**
Between Two Kings: A Novel of Anne Boleyn - **Olivia Longueville**
Phoenix Rising - **Hunter S. Jones**
Cor Rotto - **Adrienne Dillard**
The Claimant - **Simon Anderson**
The Truth of the Line - **Melanie V. Taylor**

CHILDREN'S BOOKS

All about Richard III - **Amy Licence**
All about Henry VII - **Amy Licence**
All about Henry VIII - **Amy Licence**
Tudor Tales William at Hampton Court - **Alan Wybrow**

PLEASE LEAVE A REVIEW

If you enjoyed this book, *please* leave a review at the book
seller where you purchased it. There is no better way to thank
the author and it really does make a huge difference!
Thank you in advance.

Made in the USA
Middletown, DE
20 September 2017